phpBB: A User Guide

Stoyan Stefanov
Jeremy Rogers

BIRMINGHAM - MUMBAI

phpBB:A User Guide

First published: January 2006

Published by Packt Publishing Ltd.
32 Lincoln Road
Olton
Birmingham, B27 6PA, UK.

ISBN 1-904811-91-4

www.packtpub.com

Cover Design by www.visionwt.com

This book is an abridged version of "Building Online Forums with phpBB 2", (ISBN 1904811132), focussing on a complete set of topics to get your phpBB installation up and running, and then showing you how to manage and modify your forum.

Credits

Authors
Stoyan Stefanov
Jeremy Rogers

Reviewers
Stefan Koopmanschap
Patrick O'Keefe

Technical Editor
Niranjan Jahagirdar

Editorial Manager
Dipali Chittar

Development Editor
Douglas Paterson

Indexer
Niranjan Jahagirdar

Proofreader
Chris Smith

Production Coordinator
Manjiri Nadkarni

Cover Designer
Helen Wood

About the Authors

Stoyan Stefanov is a web developer and a project manager from Montreal, Canada. He has studied in the Technical University of Sofia, Bulgaria, and McGill University, Montreal. He is a Zend Certified Engineer, with more than five years of professional web-development experience and has worked on award-winning websites for companies of all sizes—from multinational corporations to two-man startups.

He volunteers his spare time administering and programming a Bulgarian-speaking phpBB-powered online community, and contributing to the PHP community through code and articles.

Jeremy Rogers has been developing web-based applications in PHP and other languages for a little more than six years. Shortly after discovering phpBB in early 2002 and deploying it on a video-game website, he began tinkering with and learning about the internal workings of the software. Since then, he has authored dozens of expansions and tutorials related to phpBB. Jeremy currently serves the phpBB community as a phpBBHacks.com Support Team member, a capacity in which he has answered thousands of questions regarding the software, its applications, and related topics.

I would like to thank Patrick O'Keefe, for opening the doors
to a wide world that led me here.

Table of Contents

Preface

phpBB is a free, open-source Internet community application, with outstanding discussion forums and membership management. Written in the PHP scripting language, and making use of the popular MySQL database, phpBB is a standard among web-hosting companies throughout the world, and is one of the most widely used bulletin-board packages in the world. phpBB short-circuits the need for you to be a web development master in order to create and manage massive online communities.

This book is an abridged version of "Building Online Forums with phpBB 2", (ISBN 1904811132), focusing on a complete set of topics to help you set up and run your own phpBB-powered online community. In easy to follow language and with clear instructions, you will learn how to install your own system, tackle basic forum administration tasks, and customize the forum.

What This Book Covers

The book starts with an overview of phpBB and online communities. *Chapter 1* also gives some background information to phpBB, and gives you an idea of what you can achieve with phpBB with some real-life examples of phpBB-powered communities.

Chapter 2 walks you through a full installation of phpBB, including the necessary preparation work and post-installation tasks. It also looks at configuring the installation, and troubleshooting tips to get you started with your new forum and online community as quickly as possible.

After you are set up and running, *Chapter 3* and *Chapter 4* dive straight into the phpBB environment, familiarizing you with the basics of configuring your site, creating forums and users, and introducing you to the basics of phpBB administration. In order to fully understand the different features and their administration, the chapter starts with a tour of phpBB from the user and administrator points of view.

Chapter 5 looks at some more ways to customize your forum's appearance and features. Making these customizations is essential to giving your community a unique identity that makes it stand out among other online forums. The appearance of a forum is mainly controlled by phpBB's styling system, which manages the colors, images, and visual layout of the forum. In this chapter, you will learn about the basics of a phpBB 2.0 style, adding and removing styles, fixing common style installation problems, customizing styles, and adding new features, including "modifications", to the forum.

Chapter 6 completes your mastery of phpBB administration. You will learn about making your board multi-lingual, configuring avatars, managing smilies, forum, user, and group permissions, as well as the human side of forum administration—moderation, flamewars, and banning.

Conventions

In this book, you will find a number of styles of text that distinguish between different kinds of information. Here are some examples of these styles, and an explanation of their meaning.

There are three styles for code. Code words in text are shown as follows: "We can include other contexts through the use of the `include` directive."

A block of code will be set as follows:

```
CREATE TABLE phpbb_tracker (
    tracker_id mediumint(8) DEFAULT '0' NOT NULL,
    tracker1 tinyint(1) DEFAULT '0' NOT NULL,
    tracker2 varchar(40) NOT NULL,
    PRIMARY KEY (tracker_id),
);
```

When we wish to draw your attention to a particular part of a code block, the relevant lines or items will be made bold:

```
CREATE TABLE phpbb_tracker (
    tracker_id mediumint(8) DEFAULT '0' NOT NULL,
    tracker1 tinyint(1) DEFAULT '0' NOT NULL,
    tracker2 varchar(40) NOT NULL,
    PRIMARY KEY (tracker_id),
);
```

Any command-line input and output is written as follows:

```
mysqldump -u dbuser -pdbpass forums > mydump.sql
```

New terms and **important words** are introduced in a bold-type font. Words that you see on the screen, in menus or dialog boxes for example, appear in our text like this: "clicking the Next button moves you to the next screen".

> Warnings or important notes appear in a box like this.

Tips and tricks appear like this.

Reader Feedback

Feedback from our readers is always welcome. Let us know what you think about this book, what you liked or may have disliked. Reader feedback is important for us to develop titles that you really get the most out of.

To send us general feedback, simply drop an e-mail to feedback@packtpub.com, making sure to mention the book title in the subject of your message.

If there is a book that you need and would like to see us publish, please send us a note in the SUGGEST A TITLE form on www.packtpub.com or e-mail suggest@packtpub.com.

If there is a topic that you have expertise in and you are interested in either writing or contributing to a book, see our author guide on www.packtpub.com/authors.

Customer Support

Now that you are the proud owner of a Packt book, we have a number of things to help you to get the most from your purchase.

Downloading the Example Code for the Book

Visit http://www.packtpub.com/support, and select this book from the list of titles to download any example code or extra resources for this book. The files available for download will then be displayed.

The downloadable files contain instructions on how to use them.

Errata

Although we have taken every care to ensure the accuracy of our contents, mistakes do happen. If you find a mistake in one of our books—maybe a mistake in text or code—we would be grateful if you would report this to us. By doing this you can save other readers from frustration, and help to improve subsequent versions of this book. If you find any errata, report them by visiting http://www.packtpub.com/support, selecting your book, clicking on the Submit Errata link, and entering the details of your errata. Once your errata have been verified, your submission will be accepted and the errata added to the list of existing errata. The existing errata can be viewed by selecting your title from http://www.packtpub.com/support.

Questions

You can contact us at questions@packtpub.com if you are having a problem with some aspect of the book, and we will do our best to address it.

1
Introduction to phpBB

An online bulletin board in essence is an Internet-enabled version of the bulletin boards found in stores and other public areas. It's basically just a place where people leave messages for others to read. Well, the online bulletin board applications have become much more powerful and sophisticated than that, but the general principle is the same. phpBB is one of the most popular free software that implement the bulletin board idea on the Web today.

In the first chapter of this phpBB book, you will learn about:

- Online communities
- phpBB history
- phpBB development and where it's heading
- What can be achieved with phpBB, and examples of existing phpBB sites

Online Communities

An online community is a group of people who gather together on a website for some reason. This reason can be any subject of interest common to the group, like occupation, hobby, passion, or location. Such online communities are very popular, and their popularity is growing as more and more people start surfing the Web. Think about it—everyone has something he or she is passionate about. And everybody likes meeting people who share their interests. Historically, such computer-based communities existed even before the Internet; using, for example, the modem-to-modem based bulletin board systems (BBS).

An essential part of being in a community is sharing and contributing (for example, commenting on a subject or pointing out topics of interest for the group). This way, the site visitors are no longer just looking at a website that is set in stone. They are changing its face by contributing content. Today, the ability to post comments on the websites we visit has become so common that we almost expect it to be there.

Static, brochure-like sites are becoming outdated. Communities rule the Web. This is good news for both site owners and site visitors. Sites are built to be visited and used by people, and at the same time, the people are taking part in building the sites they visit. Site owners can get immediate feedback on what their visitors like or dislike, and visitors get new and fresh content on every visit. It's quite common these days that the community would not just *influence* a site owner's decisions, but even *make* the decisions through polls or open discussions. So it's not an exaggeration to say that more often than not, the success or the failure of a website is determined by the success or the failure in building an online community around the website. At the end of the day, a site is built to be used by the people, and the people have the final say if this site is worth something or not.

Building the Community—The Tools

In order to set up the place where your online community will meet, you need tools. You can invest your efforts into creating the tools yourself—assuming of course that you have expertise in web programming, server administration, and so on—or you can decide not to reinvent the wheel and can adopt a solution. That's where phpBB comes in.

There are different sorts of community-building tools out there. They can be as simple as a guestbook, or as complicated like chat systems, web logs (blogs), or mailing lists. Or they can be forums, also known as bulletin boards. The forum systems inherited and extended the bulletin board systems (BBS) from the dark pre-Internet ages, adding a web browser interface to them. phpBB belongs to the family of forum tools for building an online community.

The Name

The name consists of two parts—"PHP" and "BB". PHP is the programming language in which the software is written, and "BB" stands for "bulletin board"; it's a bulletin board tool written in the PHP programming language.

PHP itself is an abbreviation, and it stands, or at least used to stand, for Personal Home Page. PHP is no longer just a set of personal home page tools as it was in the beginning, but has grown to become a true programming language. Its abbreviation has gone one level deeper, and now recursively stands for "PHP Hypertext Preprocessor". But it's really known simply as PHP.

The Environment

In technical terms, here's what you need in order to use phpBB:

- The programming code to be executed
- A database to store information
- Web-server software, since this is a web application
- A computer to run all this!

As you already know, phpBB is coded using the **PHP** server-side programming language. Additionally in order to run, phpBB needs a database. That's where all discussions' data is stored. There are different database systems out there that phpBB can work with, but the most popular and most commonly used in today's PHP applications is **MySQL**. Finally, phpBB needs a web server and a computer running an operating system. phpBB can run on different operating systems and web servers, but it's mostly used on a **Linux** platform with the **Apache** web server.

Using the web developers' lingo, you might say that phpBB is mostly used in LAMP environments, where LAMP is an abbreviation for Linux, Apache, MySQL, and PHP. One important thing about the LAMP environment is that its components are free and open source. In practice "free and open-source" means:

- You can use the software without paying for software licenses.
- The programming code of the software is available to you if you want to modify it to better suit your needs.

Another good thing about phpBB is that it has very low requirements for the hosting server. Due to the fact that the phpBB environment consists of free software products, you can find a good and quite inexpensive hosting provider very easily. Just searching Google for "phpbb hosting" yields about a million results.

Why phpBB?

Why should you pick phpBB from all the options you have to choose from? Well, since you're reading this book, chances are you've already made up your mind, so let me just give you a few hints about how to deal with this fellow webmaster friend of yours that's running vBulletin, Phorum, or another type of system.

- phpBB is free. And it seems like it's going to stay this way. There have already been offers from companies to buy phpBB, but those were refused.

- phpBB is one of the most popular forum software. All those webmasters out there cannot be wrong. Continued usage of phpBB to power their web communities is their best testimonial.

- People know phpBB. Being so popular, it's very likely that your visitors have seen and used it already. They don't have to learn an entirely new system, and can start posting at once, feeling comfortable in a known environment.

- phpBB is mature. It has been around for more than four years of active and heavy use, which in Internet terms is a pretty long period.

- phpBB is feature rich and is open for custom feature additions. You can code your own custom features or you can use one or more of the numerous phpBB add-ons, also known as MODs or hacks, contributed by the community of phpBB users.

- phpBB's looks are customizable. You can easily change fonts and colors. You can even change the layout or use an existing layout contributed by other phpBB users.

History

James Atkinson is the creator of the software. He's the first developer and now the project manager of the phpBB project. Like a lot of other open-source projects, phpBB started as a personal project. James wanted to set up a discussion forum on his wife's site. At this time, he had two options: using a commercial package like the pioneer UBB (Ultimate Bulletin Board, written in Perl) or using the free solution named Phorum, which was written in PHP, but had a thread style James didn't like very much. So he decided to go on his own and create a UBB-like PHP-based bulletin board system.

phpBB was "born" on July 1st, 2000, at 06:45 PM. We know the exact date and time, because that's when James posted a message on an Internet forum saying that he had created a bulletin board and would like some help with the testing. A few weeks later he opened up the source code for the project, making it free and available for everyone who wanted to join in and contribute to the development.

Other enthusiasts joined, and on December 16th, 2000, the first official phpBB was released—phpBB version 1.0. After this, the release-feature requests-development-testing-release wheel started spinning for the phpBB team.

phpBB became really popular after version 2.0 was released on April 4th, 2002. This version was a complete rewrite of the source code, because the software had become much more feature rich than originally expected, and the old codebase just couldn't accommodate the new development. The interface was also completely revamped.

Development

phpBB is an open-source project and has some specifics as such:

- The developers are *volunteers* from around the world. phpBB is an example of a successful open-source project. It has an impressive team list of about 50 people, when most open-source projects have two or three.
- There's a *community* of users who often convert into collaborators.

You might be wondering how the community and the open-source nature of phpBB can help its development. There are a lot of ways, but just to name the major ones:

- Using and thus testing the software
- Reporting bugs so they can be fixed by the developers
- Contributing new features through MODs and hacks, and in this way extending the functionality
- Contributing new templates for the other phpBB admins to use
- Supporting other phpBB users with tips and advice
- Advocating and promoting phpBB, in this way increasing the size of the community

phpBB is under constant development. The work for version 3 is well underway, and in the spirit of this open-source project, the work in progress is available for preview and comments as it's developed.

Example phpBB Sites

One of the great things about phpBB is that it's highly customizable and extendable both in terms of functionality and looks. This means that:

- You can use your preferred color scheme, fonts, and overall layout.
- You can modify phpBB and develop your own feature extensions, or you can use existing modifications.

In this section, you will find a few real-life examples of how phpBB is used to power online community sites.

A Standard phpBB Layout

Let's start with an example of an out-of-the-box solution that uses the default phpBB style and the default set of features. On this example site, even the phpBB logo is left intact. This is the site of Distributed Proofreaders (`http://www.pgdp.net/phpBB2/`), a site that uses phpBB to provide a web-based method of easing the proofreading work associated with the digitization of public-domain books into Project Gutenberg e-books. By breaking the work into individual pages, many proofreaders can be working on the same book at the same time.

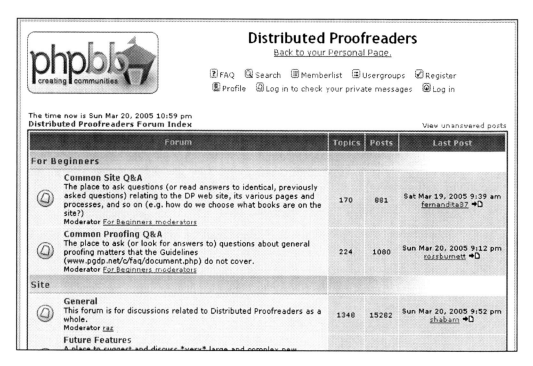

Standard Sites with Different Templates

The next examples are phpBB installations with the default feature set, but with different styles. You have a lot of options when it comes to the presentation of your board.

Instead of going with the default phpBB looks, you can find a pre-made template that better suits your needs and layout/color preferences. Or, if you can't find a template you'd like to use and you know some HTML, you can even create your own custom templates. Here are some sites that use templates different than the default one.

Mike Lothar: The personal site (`http://community.mikelothar.com/`) of one of the authors of the Packt book *Building Online Communities with phpBB 2* (ISBN: 1-904811-13-2). His chapter in that book guides you through the process of creating your own custom templates:

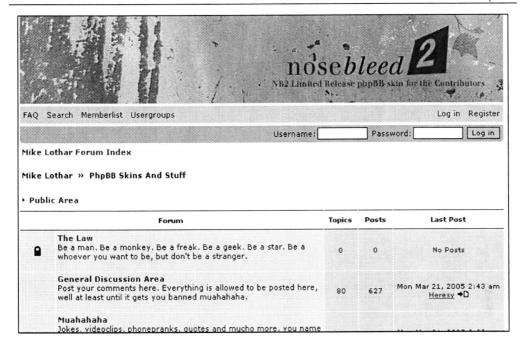

Keenspot: A bulletin board for discussing comic books
(`http://forums.keenspot.com/`):

ForumPlasma: A gaming community (http://www.forumplasma.com/):

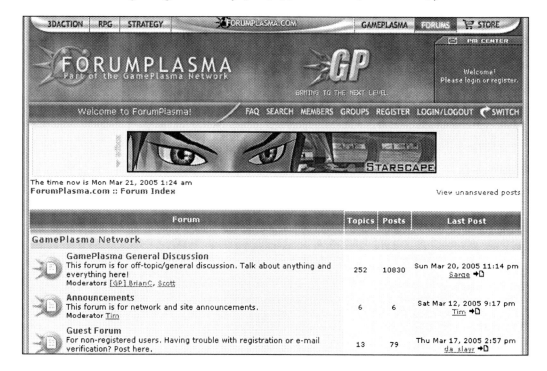

Sites with Standard Style and Modified Features

Some sites opt in for the default phpBB style, but introduce new features. These new features are often called modifications (MODs) or hacks.

You can find lots of pre-made MODs available for free download, and you can use them to enhance your board.

Dogomania forums: A community of dog owners. The site differs from the standard phpBB installation with its custom header, footer, and navigation (http://forum.dogomania.com/):

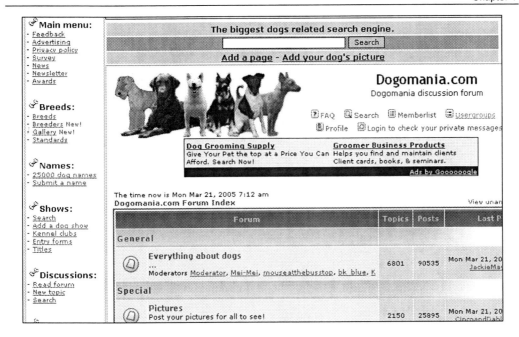

GaiaOnline

GaiaOnline is the ultimate phpBB bulletin board. The template for this site is custom, and quite a few features, customizations, and optimizations are introduced. With about 200 million posts and 1.5 million registered users, this is the biggest bulletin board on the Internet (http://www.gaiaonline.com):

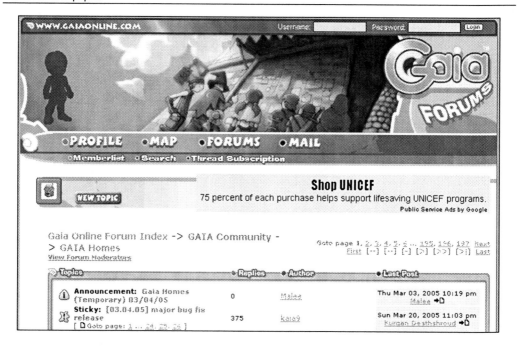

Summary

This chapter familiarized you with the phpBB solution and the problem it solves. You've learned about its history and development. You also saw a number of existing phpBB-powered community websites that can give you a hint about what you could achieve with the software. You're now ready to learn about the installation, configuration, and customization of a phpBB board. Very soon, as soon as the end of the next chapter, you'll be able to start your own community site. Let's take the trip to the world of phpBB.

2
Installing and Configuring phpBB

Now that you have a general idea of what phpBB is, it is time to install it on your server or your personal computer and to start using it. The installation process is generally not hard—phpBB has a built-in browser-based installer that makes the job much easier—but there are some pre-requisites and some details you need to be aware of before you begin. There are also some post-installation tasks that you need to perform once phpBB is installed on your system. In this second chapter of the book you will learn:

- The pre-requisites before you install phpBB
- How to download and install phpBB
- The basic post-installation tasks, along with some security tips
- Where and how to look for help when in trouble

Pre-Installation

In this section you'll find out about the phpBB server requirements, which are on the lower end (price-wise) of the server configurations offered by hosting providers. Then the section discusses some database-related topics and ends with a checklist you can use to make sure you have everything you need to start the installation process.

Requirements

phpBB is very flexible in terms of server requirements, and you have a lot of options. But let's concentrate on the configuration that is most widely used, consisting of:

- Any major operating system.
- Apache web server.

- MySQL database system, version 3.22 or higher.
- PHP version 4; PHP3 will also do, but it's recommended that you use the latest stable version.

phpBB was designed with portability in mind, so all of the requirements listed above are very flexible. Let's look at them in more detail and also see what options you have.

- **The operating system (OS)**: phpBB is OS independent. That means it can run on all sorts of operating systems—Windows, Linux, MacOS. You should not have any problem meeting this requirement and can enjoy running your forums in your preferred or most affordable environment.

- **The web server**: phpBB can run on various web servers, including the most popular Apache server and Microsoft's Internet Information Systems (IIS). If you're using a hosting service, the web server requirement won't be in the way. But if you want to install phpBB on your computer, you'll have to take care of this detail. Although describing how to install a web server is not within the scope of this book, you'll find some useful information further down.

- **The database system**: Currently supported by phpBB are MySQL 3.22 or higher (including MySQL 4.x), PostgreSQL 7.0.3, MS SQL Server (7 or 2000, directly or via ODBC), and MS Access (2000 or XP) via ODBC. Again, depending if you're installing phpBB locally or on a remote server, you'll need to either install a supported database system on your computer, or simply ask you service provider what database you have access to.

- **PHP**: In general, all PHP applications consist of files containing programming instructions that are executed by what is called a PHP interpreter. The PHP interpreter is a piece of software that you'll need to have running on the system where you want to install phpBB. If you go with a hosting service, the good news is that PHP is so popular that it would be actually harder to find a host that doesn't support it.

  PHP 4.x is the most widely used PHP version and also the most widely used for phpBB installations. As already mentioned, PHP 3.x will be sufficient to have your board running, but it's not recommended. PHP 5 is also not recommended (yet), because phpBB is not thoroughly tested on this platform, due to the fact that phpBB was developed prior to the release of PHP 5.

> phpBB will run on PHP versions 3.x and 4.x, but if you have a choice, you should aim at the latest stable PHP 4.x version.

The Attack Plan

Now that you're clear on the requirements, let's explore the options for the system to install phpBB to:

- **You have an existing web hosting service**: In this case all you need to do is contact your hosting provider and ask them if they support PHP and any of the databases listed above, preferably MySQL. If they don't, find out if they can install/enable these for you. If they still can't help you, you'll need to pick one of the remaining options.

- **You're shopping around for a good hosting provider**: The good news is that even the most inexpensive hosting packages often include PHP and MySQL support. There are lots of points to consider when choosing a hosting provider, but at the very least, browse for some independent reviews on the Web. Don't just rush into the cheapest package with huge or even unlimited bandwidth and disk space. Ask your host-to-be a question or two (for example concerning the requirements above) and judge the speed and the quality of their response. You'd want a reliable support when in need.

- **You want to install phpBB on your own computer**: Sometimes, even if you go with one of the first two options, you might still want to test your board locally. For example, if later on you want to experiment with installing or creating new styles or modifications, it would probably be easier (and definitely safer) to develop and test on your own computer *before* going live.

If you want to set up the environment on your computer, you have two options: to install all the necessary components one by one, configure them, and make them work together, or to use one of the all-in-one installations (bundles) you can find on the Internet. They usually include one downloadable installer program that takes care of installing and configuring all you need—Apache, PHP, MySQL—and often more. Such all-in-one bundles are XAMPP (http://www.apachefriends.org/en/) and others that are listed at HotScripts, for example (http://www.hotscripts.com/PHP/Software_and_Servers /Installation_Kits/).

If you want to set up your environment yourself and not make use of the bundles available out there, here's what you need to do.

Time For Action—Setting Up the Environment on Your Local Computer

1. Install the Apache web server.

> Go to http://httpd.apache.org/download.cgi. Download the latest stable 1.3.x version of the server for your operating system from the mirror closest to you geographically. Install it, and if in doubt, refer to the documentation at http://httpd.apache.org/docs/.

2. Install PHP.

> Download the latest stable 4.3.x. release for your operating system from
> `http://www.php.net/downloads.php`. Install, referring to the documentation
> (`http://www.php.net/manual/en/install.php`) as necessary.

3. Install MySQL.

> Download the latest recommended version from
> `http://dev.mysql.com/downloads/`. The documentation is just a click away at
> `http://dev.mysql.com/doc/mysql/en/Installing.html`.

4. Install phpMyAdmin (optional).

> phpMyAdmin is a free and a very popular web application for managing MySQL
> databases through a simple and intuitive browser interface. You don't need it
> absolutely, but it can make your life a whole lot easier when it comes to database
> operations. It requires PHP, but you've already installed it anyway, so you're all
> set. The latest stable version can be downloaded from
> `http://www.phpmyadmin.net/`.

While you were downloading, you've probably noticed the suggestions to download
"source" or "binaries". Download the binaries, but if you're really curious about what the
behind-the-scenes code looks like, download the source files, play around with them, and
try compiling them yourself. This, of course, will require some knowledge in C
programming. All this source code is free for use, learning, and modifications. Welcome
to the wonderful world of open-source software!

Now with a web server running PHP and MySQL (or another database system), let's take
a look at some database preparation work.

Finishing Pre-Install Touch—The Database

phpBB will need access to a database, so you'll have to use an existing database or create
a new one. Depending on whether you'll be installing on your local computer or on a
remote server, you'll have different options for setting up the database required by
phpBB; we'll take a look at those options. If you have a choice, use a new empty database
for phpBB; it makes maintenance easier.

Setting Up the Database for Local Installations

If you're installing phpBB on your personal computer, you should have no restrictions creating a new database to use with phpBB. You can do that by using phpMyAdmin or using the console (the command prompt). With phpMyAdmin, creating a new database is really easy; this is one of the first options you're presented with when you load the application. If you don't have phpMyAdmin installed, you can use the command prompt to create a new database. Let's see how to do it both ways. For the purposes the examples in this chapter, let's say your new database is named "forums".

Time For Action—Creating the Forum Database with phpMyAdmin

1. Go to your main phpMyAdmin page.
2. Enter the text forums into the Create new database field.
3. Click the Create button.

What Just Happened

You've created a new database. In the database dropdown that you see in your phpMyAdmin on the left, you will now find a new option—the "forums" database that you've just created.

Time For Action—Creating the Forum Database Using the Command Prompt

1. Access your command prompt. (Windows users, click Start, then Run, and then type cmd).
2. In the command prompt (console window), follow the path to where MySQL is installed using cd directory_name to enter a directory (cd as in "change directory") and cd .. to go back (one level up), if you've mistakenly entered a wrong directory.
3. Once you are in the directory where MySQL is installed, go to the bin directory, where you'll find several MySQL executables.
4. Type mysql -u root -p.

> This instruction means "connect to MySQL using the username root and ask me for a password". root is the default username when MySQL is installed. If you have created other MySQL user accounts, you can use one of those accounts.

5. When prompted to provide a password, hit *Enter* (*Return* on Macs). What this means is you give a blank password. Username root with a blank password is the default MySQL account. If you have changed this password, type it in.

6. You'll see a welcome message and the mysql prompt if you've successfully connected. Type CREATE DATABASE forums; and hit *Enter*. Do *not* forget the semicolon at the end.

7. If you want to verify that the database has been created, type SHOW DATABASES; and hit *Enter*. You should see your newly created database in the list.

8. That's it. Type exit, hit *Enter* and MySQL will politely say Bye to you.

9. Type exit again to close your command prompt.

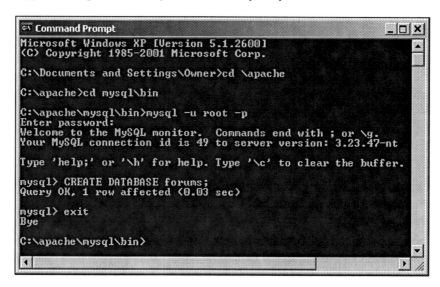

Setting Up the Database for Remote Installations

In this case the process may vary considerably depending on your specific hosting package and its limitations. Here are some possible scenarios:

- Some hosts give you one database only with a predefined name. Find out what that name is; this is the database you'll be using.

- Some hosts let you create your database(s) with phpMyAdmin installed on their server.

- Some give you a different web interface for creating a database as part of the hosting package's control panel.

- Some can give you shell access to their server. Shell access means you'll be able to use a command prompt and execute instructions (commands) on the remote server. In this case, find out from your hosting provider how to establish a shell connection to your server. After you're connected, repeat the steps for creating a database using the command prompt as previously described. This time you'll be using the database username and password given to you by your host.In order to establish a shell connection you'll need a program called a **shell client**. A popular choice is the free PuTTY telnet and SSH client (`http://www.chiark.greenend.org.uk/~sgtatham/putty/`).

Security tip: If at all possible on your host, create a new MySQL user account, give it only privileges to the new database you've just created and use it for the phpBB installation. This may seem a bit too paranoid, but the reason is that usually hosts give you one username and password only and it's good for everything—FTP, MySQL, control panel, and shell access. So the reason behind creating a new MySQL username/password combo is that if it gets revealed for some reason, the villain who has it can do only limited damage. This password is good for one database only and not FTP, shell, or control panel access.

When creating this new database user account, it's a good idea to assign only "select", "insert", "update", and "delete" privileges; the other possible privileges are not needed for the normal functioning of phpBB. The phpBB installation, though, will also require a "create" privilege and some modification installations might need "alter" or "drop" privileges. So the most security-oriented option would be to assign "select", "insert", "update", "delete", and "create" privileges to the new database user, and once the installation is completed, remove the "create" privilege.

The actual process of creating the new database user may vary, depending on your hosting provider's policies. Some might not allow it, some might give you a special interface for it, and some might give you access to phpMyAdmin. Creating a new MySQL user account using phpMyAdmin is pretty straightforward; just click the Users link on the phpMyAdmin main page and then fill out the Add form.

If you're using the command prompt for creating a new user, use the following query:

```
GRANT SELECT,INSERT,UPDATE,DELETE,CREATE
ON forums.*
TO 'mysecretusername'@'localhost'
IDENTIFIED BY 'mysecretpassword';
```

In this example, `forums` is the database name, `localhost` is the database host name, `mysecretusername` is the username to be assigned to this database user, and `mysecretpassword` is the password.

phpBB Pre-Installation Checklist

You're now ready to install phpBB. But take a minute to answer the following questions before you go on; it's just to double-check that you have everything you need:

- Do I have a web server running?
- Is my web server running PHP?
- Is my web server running MySQL or PostgreSQL or MSSQL or MS Access?
- Do I know my FTP hostname, username, and password? (This step is for remote servers only; see the note after the checklist.)
- What's my username to access the database?
- What host is this database running on? (Ask your hosting provider; it's often localhost or 127.0.0.1. In the case of ODBC, a DSN is needed instead.)
- What is the name of my database (e.g. forums)?

A note about FTP: You'll need an FTP program, also known as an *FTP client*, in order to transfer files from your computer to a remote server. There are a lot of free/trial FTP programs you can use. Just a simple Google search will yield a lot of results. Generally, using an FTP program is not much different than copying files to different locations on your local computer. The difference is that you need to establish a connection to the remote computer first. In order to do that, you need an FTP hostname, a username and a password, which you probably already have, supplied by your hosting provider.

Installation

Now that all the prerequisites have been met, let's start the installation process:

1. **Download**: Download the compressed phpBB files from http://www.phpbb.com/downloads.php selecting a compression format that you know how to decompress.

2. **Decompress**: Unzip the files to a selected directory, using your preferred compression utility (WinZip for example). If you're installing locally, unzip to a directory within your web root. The top-level directory of the phpBB directory tree will be called phpBB2.

3. **FTP**: If you're installing locally, skip this step. If you're installing on a remote server, copy the whole phpBB2 directory as-is to the remote server. You can do this easily using an FTP program to connect to your server and transfer the files.

4. **Select your phpBB root**. This step is when you need to make an important decision—where on your server you are installing phpBB and how you are naming it. The reason why this is important is because this will determine

how your users will see your board. Let's say your domain is http://www.yourdomain.com. You have the following options:

- o If you copy the phpBB2 directory and its contents to your web root and install without any modifications, your forums will be available at http://www.yourdomain.com/phpBB2.

- o You can simply rename the phpBB2 directory to something you like, say forum. In this case, your community will be located at http://www.yourdomain.com/forum.

- o You have the option of hosting the board in your web root so that it's accessible directly at http://www.yourdomain.com/ or, if you use a sub-domain, something like http://forum.yourdomain.com/. If you decide to go this way, than you need to copy the *contents* of the phpBB2 directory in your (sub)domain's web root, which is not the phpBB2 directory itself, but the files and directories that are contained within it.

For the purposes of this chapter, we'll go with the second option, http://www.yourdomain.com/forum, as it is probably the most common one.

5. config.php: You need to change the permissions for this file so that it's writable by phpBB during the installation. Go to the main directory where phpBB is installed and find the file called config.php. Change the file permissions so that it's writable by the phpBB installer scripts, or in other words, on Linux systems, chmod it to 666 (or -rw-rw-rw-). On Linux/Unix systems, chmod is a command that means "change mode", and is used to adjust file permissions. File permissions specify who can do what to a particular file. Your options to change a file's mode include:

- o If you have shell access to your Linux server, go to your phpBB directory and type chmod 666 config.php. This will do.

- o If you have FTP-only access, chances are your FTP client (the program you use for copying files to the remote server) will give you the option of chmod-ing, only you have to find it. In some FTP clients, this option is simply called chmod, in others it's under file properties or permissions.

- o If you cannot change the file permissions, don't worry. If the phpBB installer cannot write this file during the installation, you'll be given the option of downloading the config.php file on your system and then FTP-ing the file, overwriting the one already in the phpBB root.

6. **Start the phpBB installer**: Point your browser to the phpBB directory, which in our case is http://www.yourdomain.com/forum/. You'll be redirected automatically to the installation script, which is located at http://www.yourdomain.com/forum/install/install.php.

You should see a screen like the one that follows.

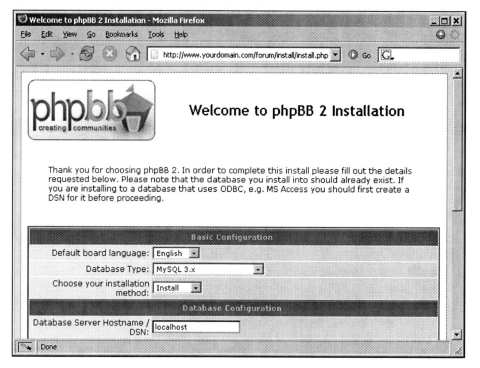

7. **Installer data form**: Complete the form that is presented on the installation screen. That's where your checklist from the previous section comes in handy. A description of the fields in this form follows, as some might not be so self-explanatory. In brief, most of the fields in this form are pre-filled by the phpBB installer; the ones you need to worry about are basically just the fields related to database name, username, password, and the administrator username, password, and email address.

Option	Setting
Default board language	Since you haven't installed additional languages yet, English is the only option. Later on if you decide to use other languages, you can always change this setting.

Option	Setting
Database Type	The database system you'll be using, most likely MySQL 4.x or MySQL 3.x
Choose your installation method	Install or Upgrade. Go with Install, since you have no previous phpBB installation.
Database Server Hostname / DSN	Usually localhost; refer to your checklist.
Your Database Name	Refer to your checklist.
Database Username	Refer to your checklist.
Database Password	Refer to your checklist again.
Prefix for tables in database	phpbb_ is the default value. After the installation, all tables in the database to do with phpBB will have this prefix in their name, such as phpbb_users, and phpbb_posts. It's not compulsory to use a prefix, but it's a nice way to tell your phpBB tables from all the rest, in case you have other non-phpBB tables in the same database. This also allows you, for example, to have two or more distinct phpBB installations that share the same database; you just need to use a different prefix for each installation. Don't use spaces in this prefix, otherwise the installer will return an error. It's a good idea to leave the default phpbb_ value for the prefix, if you don't have a reason to change it. Most of the phpBB modifications that you may want to install later on will assume this prefix.
Admin Email Address	Your email address. It will be used, for example, as a sender email address when phpBB notifies a user about a new private message. So a good idea is to supply a working email address that you check often. An email that represents your board, like admin@yourdomain.com, would be a good choice.
Domain Name	Your domain's name. The phpBB installation will probably figure it out, otherwise type it in yourself.
Server Port	The default is 80. Normally you don't need to change this value.

Option	Setting
Script path	The relative path to your installation. Normally the phpBB installer will guess it properly and you wouldn't have to change it.
Administrator Username	The administrator username is an important one. There is no default, but using Administrator is a common choice.
Administrator Password	Choose it wisely and make it difficult to guess. This option cannot be left blank.

8. **Finish installation**: Click the Install button. If everything so far was fine, you've filled out all the required data in the install form, and there were no error messages, phpBB will install successfully. Click Finish installation and move on to the post-installation tasks.

Troubleshooting the Installation

This troubleshooting guide is not a comprehensive list; it just contains some common problems that phpBB users have. If your problem is not listed here, see the last section of this chapter for guidelines on how to look for help.

Symptom

Error message: Your config file is un-writeable at present.

Reason

For some reason, step 5 of the install steps listed above was not completed. Read the description of step 5 again, but only if you need more background information on the nature of the error. Otherwise just see the solution that follows.

Solution

The phpBB installer itself will recover from this situation. Just follow the instructions on the screen.

You are given the option of downloading the config.php file the installer tried to write. Download the file, and then copy/FTP it, overwriting the config.php file that is already in the phpBB root directory.

Alternatively, you are also given the option of using the installer to FTP the file for you, provided that your version of PHP supports FTP-ing (most likely). If you want to use this option, you'll have to enter the data you normally use to connect to the server with your desktop FTP client (CuteFTP, SmartFTP, etc.). Be sure to enter the full path to where the phpBB installer can copy the config.php file. The full path is the same as that visible in your FTP client. In other words, the phpBB installer is trying to act as an FTP client for you.

Symptom

Error message: Could not connect to the database.

Reason

There can be several reasons for this message:

- You don't have a database system installed.
- The database system is installed, but it's not running.
- You didn't select the correct database type from the dropdown described in step 7.
- The database hostname/DSN is incorrect.
- The database name you provided refers to a non-existing database.
- Your username to access the database is incorrect or this database user has insufficient privileges.
- Your password to access the database is incorrect.

Solution

Read the pre-installation section again. Be sure to complete the checklist at the end with the correct data. If you're still having problems, consult the last section at the end of this chapter for an idea where you can look for help.

Symptom

Error message: The passwords you entered did not match.

Reason

This refers to the administrator password and the password confirmation you've entered at the very end of the installer form, under Admin configuration.

Solution

Be sure to enter the same password in both fields. The password cannot be blank.

Symptom

Error message: The PHP configuration on your server doesn't support the database type that you chose.

Reason 1

PHP actually supports the database system you want to use, but you didn't select it from the installer form's database type field.

Solution

Click your browser's Back button and select the appropriate database type.

Reason 2

Exactly as the message says, your PHP installation doesn't support the selected database system.

Solution

Talk to your hosting provider, or, if you're installing locally, read the PHP documentation on how to enable support for your selected database type.

Symptom

Error message: An error occurred trying to update the database
Table 'phpbb_auth_access' already exists.

Here phpbb_ is the table prefix you've typed in the installer form.

Reason 1

Although very unlikely, it may happen that in your database you have a table totally unrelated to phpBB, having the same name as a phpBB table.

Solution

This is a naming conflict. To get around this, go back and choose a different table prefix.

Reason 2

You're trying to install using a database that already contains a phpBB installation.

Solution

If you want to keep the existing installation, go back to the installer form and simply choose a different prefix. This way you're resolving the naming conflict and you'll have two phpBB installations, which use the same database.

If you don't want to keep the existing installation—for example, it was a failed installation—you have to remove all database tables created by the previous installation. Which tables to remove? You can tell by their prefix. Use the friendly phpMyAdmin to remove those tables, or if you can't use it, connect to MySQL on the command prompt as described earlier in this chapter, and delete the tables manually. To do so, you need to use the DROP TABLE syntax, which is actually very simple but also a bit dangerous because it deletes a whole database table and its contents permanently.

Time For Action—Deleting phpBB Tables using phpMyAdmin

1. Load the phpMyAdmin main page.
2. Select forums from the dropdown on the left-hand side. forums is the database name; use your database name if different.
3. On the right, where all the tables are displayed, check the box next to each table you want to delete. You can also use the Check All link to select all the tables in this database.
4. Select Drop from the action options.

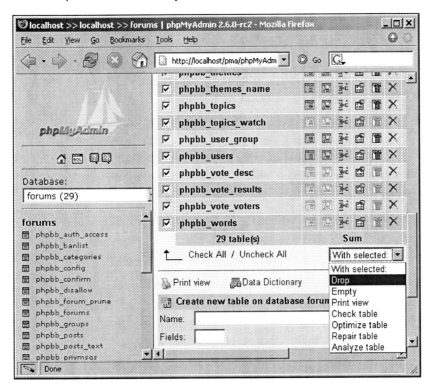

Time For Action—Deleting phpBB Tables Using the Command Prompt

1. Connect to MySQL using the console as described in the pre-install section.
2. Once you're connected to MySQL, change the database in use, by using \u forums, where forums is the name of your database.
3. List all tables with SHOW TABLES; and then delete them one by one using DROP TABLE table_name_here;.

Alternatively if you're sure there are no tables that you need in this database—that there's nothing but some no-good phpBB tables from a failed installation—you can do it in one shot: after connecting to MySQL, type DROP DATABASE forums;.

This will delete the whole database. Permanently! So be careful. You need to recreate it again for the next installation.

> Deleting tables and databases is a one-way process, meaning you can't go back. So think twice before you delete anything. Think about taking backups when you're in doubt before destroying some tables.

Here's a MySQL query that allows you to quickly back up a table:

```
CREATE TABLE 'new_table_name'
SELECT * FROM 'table_to_back_up';
```

This will create a new table, called new_table_name in the same current database, and the new table will have the same structure and content as the table named table_to_back_up.

If you want to back up a table in a different database, you can use:

```
CREATE TABLE 'new_database'.'new_table_name'
SELECT * FROM 'source_database'.'table_to_back_up';
```

Post-Installation Tasks

After you've installed phpBB, you need to perform a few post-install operations, namely to delete unneeded directories and to set some basic configuration options.

Time For Action—Deleting Unneeded Directories

1. Connect to your server via FTP (skip this step for local installations).
2. Go to the directory where phpBB is installed.
3. Delete the install and contrib directories.
4. (Optionally) delete the docs directory as well.

What Just Happened?

After a successful installation, when you visit your new phpBB forum's homepage you'll get a hint about your post-install tasks. You're advised to delete the install and contrib directories, because leaving them on the server is considered a security risk, so big that phpBB won't even run if it detects their presence.

The doc directory can be deleted as well if you like; it's not a security threat, but can save some disk space.

Basic Configuration

After the unneeded directories are deleted, you can access your new and shiny bulletin board that you just installed. Great! It works!

Now it's a good idea to familiarize yourself a bit with the administration panel. And you can do this right away by editing some general configuration variables.

Time For Action—Initial Configuration Using the Administration Panel

1. Load your bulletin board in the browser, i.e. visit http://www.yourdomain .com/forum. It looks like the following screenshot:

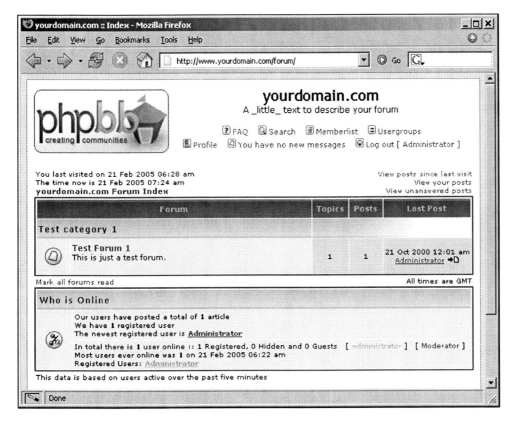

2. Log in using the form at the bottom of the page. Depending on how the installation ended, you may be logged in already. If you're not, use the administrator username and password that you selected during the installation.

3. Click the Go to Administration Panel link; it is located at the bottom of every page.

4. Click the Configuration link found under the General Admin section in the left-hand menu.

5. Edit the fields as needed (discussed shortly).

6. Click Submit when done.

What Just Happened?

You successfully logged in to your administration panel, the place for managing your phpBB-powered bulletin board. You loaded the general configuration settings form and saved the settings.

Most of the fields in this form are pre-filled with values that are just fine as the phpBB installer set them, but some are better if edited. What follows is a list of fields of interest:

General Board Settings

Site name: A friendly name for your site: often, the domain name. It will appear at the top of every page. The default is yourdomain.com, and you can see it in action in the previous screenshot.

Site description: A brief description of what the site is about, preferably not more than six to seven words. It will appear at the top of every page and is not required. Again, look at the previous screenshot to see the default value A _little_ text to describe your forum.

Enable account activation: This refers to the way new users are accepted. There are three options:

- The users are accepted right away, as soon as they sign up (this is the default option).

- They have to confirm their subscription by clicking a link received by email. This way they confirm their wish to become members and also authenticate that they are the owners of the email address supplied during registration. This is probably the most used option.

- The members' sign-up applications need to be reviewed and approved by an administrator.

System Timezone: The time zone where your community is mainly located. It's a default value that every member can overwrite.

Enable GZip Compression: Enabling this option will cause all pages to be compressed when sent from the server and decompressed after they are received by the user's computer if the user's browser supports compression. If it doesn't, the page won't be compressed by the server. This results in a faster working site and uses less bandwidth, but increases the server load because of the overhead of compressing every page that is served.

Cookie settings

Cookie name: Normally you don't change this. You might need to alter this value only if you host more than one forum under the same domain name. If this is the case, you can use a different cookie name for each installation.

Cookie secure: Enable this option if your site runs on Secure Socket Layer (SSL); in other words if your pages are displayed using the secure HTTPS protocol, instead of just HTTP.

Session length [seconds]: Determines how long the user session "lives" before it's deleted. It's a security-related setting, which determines how many seconds users can stay inactive (not visiting any board page) before they are logged out by phpBB.

Avatar Settings

Avatar refers to those little member-specific graphics that appear in the posts below a member's username. You have three ways to provide this functionality:

- Enable gallery avatars: Users can select from a number of predefined graphics that you upload to a specified directory.
- Enable remote avatars: Users can put links to graphics that they find on the Internet, stored on other servers.
- Enable avatar uploading: Users can upload graphics to your server.

Avatar Storage Path: Where the uploaded avatars are stored; the default is images/avatars, which translates to `http://www.yourdomain.com/forum/images/avatars/`.

Avatar Gallery Path: Where the pre-defined graphics are stored; the default is images/avatars/gallery, which translates to `http://www.yourdomain.com /forum/images/avatars/gallery/`.

COPPA Settings

COPPA stands for Children's Online Privacy Protection Act. Basically it requires parents' written consent if their children are to become members of your forums. For more information, see phpBB user guide and `http://www.coppa.org`.

Email Settings

Admin Email Address: The email address that you provided during the installation.

Email Signature: This will be appended to every email phpBB sends on your behalf, such as private message notifications, topic-watch notifications, etc. Use your imagination to come up with friendly message footers to your members.

Use SMTP Server for email: You have the option of using an SMTP server to send mail, instead of the native PHP mail function. Some hosts disable the PHP mail function because of the danger of unethical clients misusing it (to send spam). If this is the case, you need to use an SMTP server to send the mails. Your Internet service provider (ISP, the one you use to connect to the Internet) has most likely given you access to an SMTP server to send emails (with Microsoft Outlook, for example). You can use this SMTP server for your bulletin board. You can also use this option if you install phpBB on your own PC and don't have a mail server set up.

Setting Up the avatars Directory

If you're allowing members to upload avatars to your server, you have to make the directory that stores them writable. The file permissions (on a Linux machine) need to be 777. Using the same methods for changing the file permissions as we used for config.php in the pre-install section, change the permissions to 777 for the image/avatars directory or wherever you decided to store members' avatars.

Security Tips

Making sure that your board is as secure as possible should always be a concern. Here are some tips that can help you get started.

Administrator Password

Make your administrator password difficult to guess. It's a very important password, so you wouldn't want other people to guess it and play around with your board. This is also true for any moderators you decide to assign later on. Remind them to change their passwords to something really hard to guess. For example, using the same password as the username is definitely not advisable. Be creative and go with something like y0u11n3v3rgue$$ (read "you'll never guess") and wh00p3375 (read "whoopee 75"). It's also a good idea to change this password regularly and to use it only for this board (not for other services like Hotmail and the like).

Disallow Remote Connections to the Database

Remote connections allow you to access your database from a remote location. For instance, from your local machine you can query the database that is running on the remote hosting server. This definitely has benefits—for example for making local backups of the data in the remote database—but it can be a security risk. If the username and password to access the database are somehow revealed, then if the remote connection is enabled, an intruder can access your data from his or her computer. If the remote connection is disabled, the hacker will have to have access to the remote server in order to be able to connect to your database. Additionally with remote connection enabled, the potential hacker can try to guess what your password is by trying different combinations until he or she is connected.

Some hosting providers let you enable/disable remote connections, while some don't allow remote connections at all. Check what your situation is and (unless you have a very good reason) make sure the remote connection is disabled.

MySQL Account

Use a new MySQL account (or a new account for any other database you might be using for that matter) for the bulletin board. This was described in more detail in the pre-install section of this chapter.

config.php

After you change the permissions of the config.php file (described in the pre-installation section) so that it's writable by all, and you install phpBB, it's time to revert back. Using the exact same methodology as described before, change the permissions to 664.

Here is a more visual description of the config file after the chmod 664 config.php command. This is a screenshot from an FTP client for Windows.

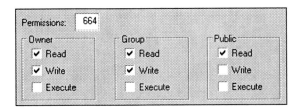

.htaccess Protection for the Administration Panel

A little extra layer of protection for the admin panel can be the setting of an .htaccess directory protection. .htaccess is a file that can contain a number of instructions for the Apache web server that are applicable for the directory where the .htaccess file is and to all sub-directories. Setting up .htaccess protection will result in an additional username/password window that will be displayed when you enter the admin panel. Setting up the protection may not be a trivial task, and there are quite a few tutorials that can help you with this available on the Web. .htaccess documentation can be found on the Apache website at http://httpd.apache.org/docs/howto/htaccess.html.

It's possible that your hosting provider gives you access to an easier interface (a control panel) that can help you set up the protection.

So using .htaccess directly or through a friendlier interface you can protect the admin sub-directory within the root phpBB directory using a username and password different than the "normal" administration password. This way you're making it harder for potential intruders as they have two different username/password pair to deal with.

Finding Help

Remember how we spoke about the huge community of phpBB users? Well, these are the people that can help you out if you have a problem that you cannot figure out. On phpBB.com, there is a support section that contains "static" articles such as the user guide, the knowledge base, and the FAQ, and there's also the community section (that is not surprisingly powered by phpBB) where phpBB users from around the globe share their experience. The same sort of community of users you can find on phpBBHacks.com.

When you encounter a problem, don't panic; you're not alone, and chances are someone has had and resolved the exact same problem, and this individual is most likely to share the resolution. So it's very probable that the question you have has already been asked and answered. All you need to do is find it. If you can't find the resolution you need, post your question on the bulletin board, but make sure you search first.

Then even though you've found your answer, don't leave right away. You could dawdle for a while and help others with problems that you know how to fix.

Summary

We've walked a long way in this chapter: setting up the different components required to have phpBB running, doing some database preparation work, downloading phpBB, and installing it. You also have an idea now of the essential phpBB configuration options and how to make your board more secure.

At this point you have the knowledge and know-how to start up your community website. Today!

3
User Experience: Visitors

In the previous chapters you learned about what phpBB is and how to install it. It is time now to take a closer look at how it actually works and the kind of features it offers to users, moderators, and administrators.

In this chapter you will learn how phpBB works from a visitor's perspective.

As more and more people join your online community, chances are that they'll start asking questions about some of the board features. You should be able to guide them and respond to their concerns if you want to be a good, understanding, and helpful host to the community. That's why it's a good idea to know in detail how your phpBB-powered forum works.

If you've just jumped from the previous chapter, you may be still logged in as an administrator. Log out and let's get started with the tour of the new forum walking in visitor's shoes.

Overview

If somebody hits the forum you've just created following the steps from the previous chapter, they are very likely to see something like the following:

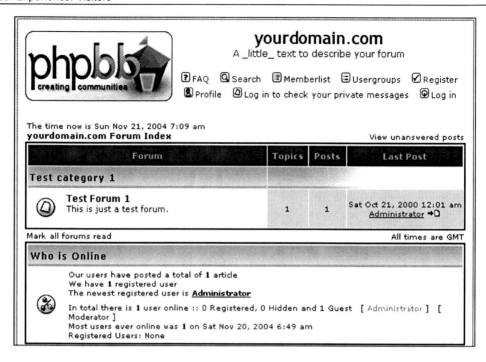

This screenshot shows how phpBB gets shipped, with all defaults and a test posting in a test forum. The only registered user of the board is the admin user that you created while installing. At the top of the screen, next to the phpBB logo, there's a set of links that go together with some small icon images. These links represent the main navigation of the forum. One of the links is the link to register and become a member of the community. Off we go!

Registration

There are three steps to the registration procedure—reading and accepting the registration terms, filling out the user profile form, and (optionally) a registration confirmation by email.

Step 1

When the visitors select the Register link from the top menu, they are presented with the "Registration Agreement Terms". There are three options they can choose from:

- **Accept the terms and be 13 years old or older**: This option triggers the standard registration procedure.

- **Accept the terms and be younger than 13 years**: This option is the same as the one above with one more addition. In compliance with COPPA (Children's Online Privacy Protection Act of 1998) regulations, a parent or guardian needs to send a standard form to you, the forum administrator, by mail or email. This form grants permission for the child to participate in the forums. A blank COPPA form is sent by phpBB to the email address supplied during the registration.

- **Don't agree to the terms**: Choosing this option aborts the registration process and the visitor is redirected to the main forum page.

Step 2

When the visitor accepts the phpBB terms, the registration form is displayed. The exact meaning of each of the fields in this registration/profile forms will be described shortly. For now let's concentrate on the absolutely required fields:

- Username
- Valid email address
- Password and password confirmation

Step 3

After all the information is filled out, the user clicks Submit. If there are validation errors, like incorrect syntax for email address or password mismatch, information about the error will be displayed at the top of the form. On an error-free and successful registration, a "thank you" screen is displayed. Depending on how the board is configured (see the Email Address field's explanation in the table shown in the *Editing Your Profile* section that follows), the thank-you screen might advise the users to check their email for a confirmation message in order to complete the registration.

Logging In

After successful registration, the user can log in using the form at the bottom of the forum's front page.

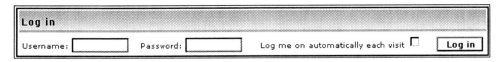

There's a checkbox next to the password field that says Log me on automatically each visit. Users should be careful when using this convenience, especially on shared computers. You as an administrator should be even more careful on using this option, as terrible things can happen if "The Bad Guy" takes over your account. Think about who else might be using your computer—family, visiting friends, etc.

Editing Your Profile

Logged-in users can edit their original profile created during registration. If they click the Profile link in the top navigation menu, they are presented with a profile form that is actually the same as the registration form, except for two things:

- The username is not editable. The Administration Panel allows for a configuration where the users *can* change their usernames, but this is not the default option, and for a good reason. Giving users the opportunity to change their identity means that it will become difficult for people to tell who's who in your community.

- There are now three password fields: one for the old password, one for the new password, and one for confirming the new password. These fields are normally left blank, and are used only if the user wants to change the password.

OK, let's revise what we've learned so far about user profiles with a simple exercise.

Time For Action—Creating and Editing "The Dude" Profile

1. Go to the homepage of your forum and select Register from the top navigation menu.
2. On the Accept terms page, select I am over 13...
3. Fill out the form using username The Dude, password test and an email address of yours. Leave everything else as it is.
4. Click the Submit button.
5. So far the registration is successful. Visit the homepage again. You will see The Dude under Who is Online, shown as The newest registered user.

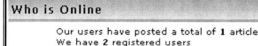

Who is Online

Our users have posted a total of **1** article
We have **2** registered users
The newest registered user is **The Dude**

In total there is **1** user online :: 0 Registered, 0 Hidden and 1 Guest
Most users ever online was **1** on Sat Nov 20, 2004 6:49 am
Registered Users: None

6. Now go to your email inbox and check your email. You should see a Welcome to yourdomain.com Forums message. This message, depending on the board configuration discussed earlier, will either tell you that you're now a member, or will provide you with a link to activate and finalize your membership application. Welcome aboard!

7. Go back to the board homepage. Scroll down to the login form. Enter The Dude as a username and the test password and press Log in. After a successful login, you'll see The Dude in the list of registered users online.

Who is Online

Our users have posted a total of **1** article
We have **2** registered users
The newest registered user is **The Dude**

In total there is **1** user online :: 1 Registered, 0 Hidden and 0 Guests
Most users ever online was **1** on Sat Nov 20, 2004 6:49 am
Registered Users: The Dude

8. Look at the main navigation links at the top and select Profile. The profile form is displayed.
9. In the blank signature field, type in the following: Humans are not proud of their ancestors, and rarely invite them round to dinner. - Douglas Adams. Leave everything else as is.
10. Click Submit to save your amended profile.

What Just Happened?

You have successfully registered a new profile, logged in, and edited this profile. This user is now ready to post.

Understanding the meaning behind the user profile fields is a key to many phpBB features, so here's a detailed description. Take your time to learn about those fields; you're going to see them time and time again in different areas of your forum.

Field name	Description
Registration Information	
Username*	Selected username. Spaces and special symbols are allowed with the exception of the quotation mark ("). At most 25 characters are allowed.

Field name	Description
E-mail address*	User's email address. The forum can be configured to request a registration confirmation by email in order to activate a user account. If such confirmation is required, an email is sent to the address provided in this field. Many phpBB administrators opt for email confirmation just to make sure that users enter valid email addresses. This has a very good reason—if you don't require the email confirmation and users register with fake email addresses, you'll start receiving lots of bounced messages to your admin email address. Why these bouncing messages? Well, phpBB will send emails on your account (you'll be the sender), for private-message notifications, topics-watch notifications, and so on, and on mail-delivery failures due to wrong recipient addresses, these mails bounce back to the sender.
Password*	Anything is acceptable as a password, including single letters, although such simple passwords are really *not* recommended.
Confirm password*	phpBB requests the password to be confirmed just for the users to verify that they've entered their intended password correctly. A note about the passwords: they are encrypted before they are saved to the database using the MD5 one-way encryption algorithm. In plain English: there's no way for a saved password to be retrieved; at least the modern computer algorithms are not capable of doing it. This means that only the users know their passwords. If a user forgets a password, there's a procedure to create a new password, but none to restore the old one.

Profile Information

As the form says, this section of the registration contains information that is publicly viewable by all community members, even those that are not registered. Part of it accompanies every post the user writes, part of it is only displayed when somebody accesses the user profile page. This section contains, for example, user data about their ICQ, AOL, MSN, and Yahoo! Messenger services and some other personal data.

There is a special field called signature. The text in this field is appended to the bottom of every post made by the user. It can contain links, URLs, and formatting, and is often used to add a touch of personality. People use it for various reasons like favorite wisdom quotes, funny quotes, or self-advertising. The way people use it can sometimes vary depending on what the community is about. On some rare occasions, it can actually be used for its original purpose—to contain the name of the poster or anything that looks like a real signature. The way to format a signature is the same as that to format a normal posting, which will be discussed a bit later.

Field name	Description
Preferences	
Always show my e-mail address	Selecting "Yes" will reveal the user's email address in the posts and in the profile. Selecting "No" would still allow other members to send email to this user, but without knowing the exact email address. They can do so by using a specially designed phpBB email interface.
Hide your online status	If "Yes" is selected, when this user is logged in, the username will not be listed in the "Who is Online" area on the front page of the forum. Many people go with this option for privacy reasons. Hidden users are displayed when logged in as an admin, though.
Always notify me of replies	On selecting "Yes", phpBB will send an email to the user every time somebody replies to a topic created by this user or a topic where the user has posted. This can be unselected on a per-posting basis.
Notify on new Private Message	On selecting "Yes", phpBB will send an email when the user receives a private message.
Pop up window on new Private Message	On selecting "Yes", when the user is currently logged in and receives a private message, a new browser window will pop up to the user, notifying of the new message.
Always attach my signature Always allow BBCode Always allow HTML Always enable Smilies	These four "Always" fields refer to corresponding checkboxes when the user writes a posting. If they are checked, the corresponding checkboxes will be checked by default, but still can be changed on a per-posting basis.
Board Language	The language for the forum. English is the only language that is shipped with the default installation, but the good news is that there are more than 50 other translations that are available. Chapter 6 explains how you can add new languages to your board.

Field name	Description
Board Style	Here the user selects how the board will look like for them. "subSilver" is the default and only board style, but shortly you'll find about how to add more styles or customize them or even create your very own!
Timezone	The users can select the time zone they are in, so that all date/time data displayed on the board is converted to their local time.
Date format	Users can configure the way the date/time data is presented to them, using the formatting options of the `date()` PHP function. There are quite a few options: details can be found in the PHP manual entry located at `http://www.php.net/date`.
	By default, the dates will be displayed like "Sat Nov 21, 2004 1:01 pm", but this can be changed to something like "2004-11-21 13:01" or "21st of November, 2004 at 01:01 pm" or whatever the user is most comfortable with.

Posting

Posting messages is the main activity in a bulletin board; everything else is a more or less just additional features. So it's a good idea to know all the details about posting.

Anatomy of a Posting

Let's see what a posting looks like, and what different elements it is composed of:

The *Author information* box consists of author's nickname, joined-in date, number of posts, and location. It can also contain the avatar image, rank, and rank image, but these are not enabled by default. Ranks and avatars are discussed a bit later.

Post meta information consists of one tiny post graphic, date/time stamp, and post subject. This teeny tiny graphic (▢) is so small that most people won't even notice it, and even if they do, they would think it's just an ornament. But it's in fact a functional graphic; it's an exact link to this post. It's not very likely that someone would want to go to the post they are reading at the moment, but this can be very useful when you want to give a link to a specific post, as opposed to a link to the topic in general. To get the exact URL of a posting, right-click this miniature graphic and copy the URL that it links to. The graphic can also be different in color, which has a meaning. In the default phpBB template, an orange-colored box denotes that it's an unread post, whereas a white-gray box means that user has already read this post.

The *Actions area* contains buttons for the actions available to the user for this posting. The quote button is always there, and it looks like this: `quote`. Another action button that can be available is the edit button, which looks like this: `edit`. Whether the edit button is available depends on the user privileges, but in the default phpBB forum configuration, an author can edit his or her postings and a moderator can edit everybody's postings. The author can also have a delete action, depending on the privileges and the specific posting. The default phpBB configuration allows the author of the post to delete it only if there are no more posts after that. Moderators have access to all action buttons—quote, edit, delete, and the button to view the poster's IP address. The *Post text* area contains the actual text of the message and the *signature* area contains the user's signature in his/her profile.

The *Top link* is just a "Back to the top" link leading to the beginning of the current page.

The *Contact author options* area at the very least contains a button to access the author's profile and a button to send the author a **private message** (**PM**). This area can also contain other information as entered in the profile: the email address, ICQ number, MSN messenger ID, web address, and so on. The nice thing about the ICQ button is that it will show the ICQ status of the author (online or offline) provided, of course, that the author is allowing the status to be viewed in the ICQ settings.

Replying

A reply is a new posting in an existing discussion topic. It's initiated by clicking the post reply (`postreply`) button located at the top and the bottom of a topic listing. A reply can also be initiated by clicking the Quote action button, mentioned earlier, located in a post's actions area. In this case, the post body will be pre-filled with the quoted posting.

Here's the interface for posting a reply:

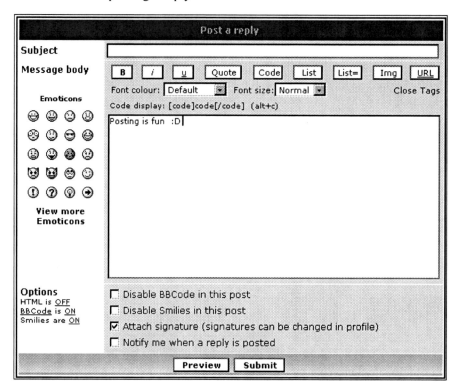

The only thing the user really needs to worry about on this form is the message body. Everything else is optional. Here are some more details about the posting interface:

- The subject (if entered) will appear in the post's meta information box (see the *Anatomy of a Posting* section)

- There are formatting options that use the so-called **BB Code (BB tags)**, where BB stands for **bulletin board**. The formatting options empower the users to improve the looks of a posting (or sometimes even ruin it).

- Emoticons (mostly known as smilies) are those cute little images that help the users add a touch of personal and informal look to their postings. Clicking one of these graphics on the left will insert its textual representation in the message-body field. For example, if you click ☺, you'll see :D inserted in the textbox, as shown in the preceding screenshot.

- The blue text View more Emoticons is actually a link to a new window popup with more smilies to choose from. This link is something people often miss and then start asking you why on earth would you hide from them this Mr.

Green icon ⊕ that everybody else seems to be using all the time. The explanation is that it's there, but is only accessible through the View more Emoticons popup.

- The options section, located below the message body, contains the checkboxes we mentioned a bit earlier; their default values are defined in the user's profile.

- Clicking on the Preview button will show the message body exactly the way it'll look when posted. It's always a good idea to use this feature.

- If the board configuration allows unregistered visitors to post, they'll see an additional field above all the rest, and this will be a required field to enter a username.

- Below the posting form, there is a listing of the latest previous postings (not displayed in the previous screenshot). This makes it easier for the post's author to recall what others have said before.

Starting a New Topic

Starting a new topic is very similar to posting a reply in an existing one. It's initiated by clicking the new topic (new topic) button. The form is very similar to the one we just saw, except that Subject is a required field, and there are fields to include a poll that will go together with the topic.

Some more topics of interest about the polls:

- When starting a new topic, uses can set a poll question, multiple answers (at least two), and the number of days before the poll expires.

- Once the poll expires, visitors can still see the results of the poll, but can no longer vote.

- Setting the number of expiration days to 0 (or leaving it blank) will cause the poll to be always accessible for voting (an **eternal poll**).

- Creating a poll requires a separate privilege that can be restricted from the admin panel, but it's allowed by default.

Formatting a Posting

Users can format postings by using a small set of instructions (BB tags). When posting, you insert these tags in the post body, and when you view a post, the tags are processed to produce the desired formatting. If you know some basic HTML tags, chances are you'll have a pretty good idea of how the BB tags work and you can start typing them almost right away.

If you don't know either HTML or BB tags (and most of your visitors won't know them), don't worry; you don't have to learn this whole new secret code by heart. phpBB has an intuitive interface to guide you through this almost as easily as using a word-processing software. Just looking at the formatting toolbar should make most of the options clear.

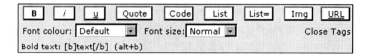

There are two ways to apply formatting: you can either type the tags out, or you can select the word or phrase you want to format and then click the appropriate button from the toolbar. Unfortunately, due to different JavaScript support in the different browsers, the second option is not available in some browsers or platforms. But the good news is that about 95% of all Internet users will have access to this feature, because they'll be using a browser that supports it.

There is always an **opening BB tag** that shows where to start the formatting and a **closing BB tag** that shows where the formatting should end. The opening tag is of the form [tag], and the closing tag, of the form [/tag]. Let's take a look at the bold tag, as it's probably the tag that's used the most. If you want to bold the word "fun" in the sentence "Posting is fun", you type (or use the toolbar to produce the same result) "Posting is [b]fun[/b]". These tags might look scary if this is your first acquaintance with them, but are really easy once you get used to them.

You know that you can apply this formatting by typing the sentence, selecting the word "fun", and then clicking the B icon. There is another way of using the toolbar to do this:

1. Type Posting is.
2. Click the B icon (this will insert the opening [b]).
3. Type fun.
4. Click the B icon again (this will insert the closing [/b]).

Unlike the selection method for formatting (described previously), the scenario above will work in almost any browser that knows at least something about JavaScript. After step 2 above, the B icon will get an asterisk, indicating that there is an opened [b] tag that's not yet closed. On completion of step 4, the asterisk will disappear.

Images can be inserted into your postings by using the [img] tag, assuming that the image is available on the Internet, i.e. you know its web address that starts with something like http://. You can also put web links into the postings, using the [url] tag, although phpBB is smart enough to guess when you have a web link in your posting and will automatically display it as a clickable link.

You can consult the phpBB guide for more detailed information on the BB tags, but let's first see an example to get a pretty good idea of how the tags work.

If you look at the earlier screenshot, which shows the formatting toolbar, you'll notice that it looks like three distinct lines (or rows), containing respectively:

- Formatting command buttons, like B for bold, I for italics, etc.

- Two dropdowns containing font formatting and a Close Tags link. This link will close all currently opened tags (assuming they were opened from the toolbar, not typed). For example, if you type Posting is, click the B button followed by the I button, type fun, and finally click Close Tags, you'll get the result: Posting is [b][i]fun[/i][/b]. Clicking Close Tags has given the same results as clicking I and then B to close the tags you've already opened.

- The third line in the toolbar contains tips on how to use the BB tags. If you place your mouse over a toolbar icon, you'll see that the contents of the tips line change to reflect the button's function. The preceding illustration had the mouse cursor hovering over the B button. In brackets, a tip shows a keyboard combination that can be used for formatting. This combination has the same effect as clicking a toolbar button, and can help you post faster using just the keyboard and not even worrying about moving your hand from the keyboard to the mouse, and then moving the mouse to the desired icon.

  The result from the example can even be achieved using just the keyboard: type Posting is, hold the *Alt* key (the Apple key for Mac users), press *B*, press *I*, release *Alt*, type fun, hold *Alt*, press *I*, and then press *B*.

Time For Action—Formatting a Post

1. You already know how to use the bold and italics formatting tags, but this time let's also add **underlining**. Use your preferred method (the toolbar or the keyboard or simply type the tags yourself) in order to produce the following BB code: Posting is [b][i][u]fun[/u][/i][/b]!.

2. The next thing is the **quoting**. Normally you would use the Quote action button when replying, but it doesn't hurt to know how to do it manually:

   ```
   I can quote other posters like this:
   [quote="The Dude"]For my name is The Dude...[/quote]
   ```

3. Now we take a look at the [code] tag, which is mostly used when people **paste programming code** into their postings, but can be used for other purposes like better aligning in a table-like manner, because it uses a fixed-width font. Type:

   ```
   I can write "phpBB" using binary:
   [code]01110000 01101000 01110000 01000010 01000010[/code]
   ```

4. Next, the **listings**. Listings use the [list] tag to mark the beginning and the end of a listing, and use the asterisk [*] for a listing item. The listing start tag can take parameters like 1 or A. Try this:

```
And I can list stuff like this:
[list][*]one[*]two[/list]
or even enumerate, like this
[list=1][*]first[*]second[/list]
```

5. Then add an **image** using the [img] tag and the web address of a known image, as follows:

```
I can use images:
[img]http://www.packtpub.com/images/Packt.png[/img]
```

6. Now **links**. Links are inserted using the [url] tag, where there are two possible scenarios. Try them both as shown here:

```
Links: [url]http://www.packtpub.com[/url], fancy links:
[url=http://www.packtpub.com]Packt Publishing[/url]
```

7. And finally, the [color] and the [size] tags. Their start tags take parameters like [color=black], [color=blue], [size=7], etc. Try the following to get a better idea:

```
and [color=red]different [/color][color=green]colors [/color]and
[size=18]font [/size][size=9]sizes[/size]!
```

What Just Happened

Click the Preview or Submit button, and you'll see what you just did. It should look like the following screenshot.

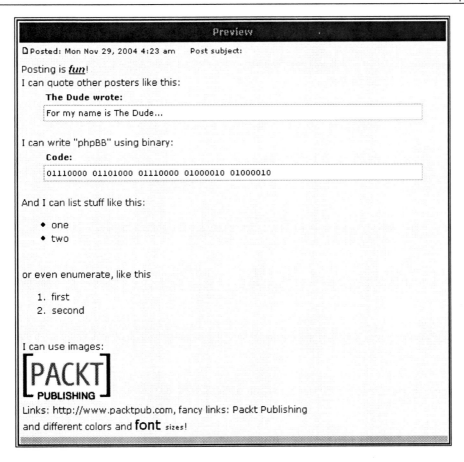

Congratulations! You've just formatted a posting using almost all of phpBB's formatting capabilities!

Editing a Posting

Users are allowed to edit their own postings. Again this is the default phpBB configuration and can be changed from the Administration Panel. Users edit their postings by using the Edit link located in the actions area.

After a posting has been edited, a small print message appears at the bottom of the posting, advising other users that this posting has been altered. The message goes like:

Last edited by The Dude on Fri Nov 26, 2004 8:02 am; edited 1 time in total

This message always appears, with only one exception; it will not appear if the posting was edited *before* another user has posted in the same topic.

Deleting a Posting

Users are allowed to delete their own postings but only if it's the last posting in the discussion topic. As soon as a reply is posted (even by the same user) the deletion of a posting is no longer possible.

Postings are deleted by using the delete action icon (⊠) located in the post's actions area.

Searching

Pretty soon your forums will be full of topics that will span more than one topics-listing page. This will make it a bit difficult to locate a specific older topic. phpBB's search feature comes to the rescue here. It's accessible through the Search top-navigation link. The search form gives you many options to find your topic of interest, such as which forum to search, how to display the results, and so on.

Chances are you and your members will ignore most of the search options in your searches. After all, we are so used to simple search boxes like Google's, for example, that we rarely look for other options. But there is one simple option here that can help you a lot. This option is Search for all terms. It helps when you search using more than one word. Unlike Google, where the results will be narrowed when you add more words, phpBB will search for each individual word and return more results (broadening the search as opposed to narrowing it). For example, if you search for milk chocolate, you'll get all results for milk and chocolate, which is probably not what you want. However, when you check the Search for all terms option, the search will return only those posts where both words can be found.

You can also use the wildcard (*) for searching a part of a word. For example *late will return postings containing the words chocolate and late.

Sending and Receiving Private Messages (PM)

One neat phpBB feature is that users can communicate privately with each other *outside* the public board area, through private messages (PM). (PM is also used as a verb, as in "Please PM me".) PMs work very similarly to the normal email we're all used to. The interface for writing a PM is the same as for writing a posting, except there is a field for the recipient's username at the top. Also, you can look up a username if you're not sure about the spelling.

There are the following private message boxes:

- **Inbox**: Stores all incoming messages, just like in a normal email mailbox.
- **Sentbox**: Contains all messages that you've sent to other members.

- **Outbox**: Temporarily contains those messages that you've sent but which have not yet been read by the recipient. You can edit or delete messages in the outbox. As soon as the recipient reads the message, the sender can no longer amend it. At this point the message is final. Sometimes it can so happen that a user receives an email and a pop-up window notification about a new PM and when this user goes to the inbox, there are no new messages. This does not happen very often, because the ability to edit or delete messages in the outbox is a somewhat hidden feature that most people are not aware of. But in any event, be prepared to answer the users' queries as to why they receive notifications but no messages.

- **Savebox**: Stores sent or received messages. You can move messages to this box from the other boxes. This is useful as storage for keeping some important messages that you want to have separated from the others so that you don't accidentally delete them. The savebox can also be used to offload the other boxes when they are reaching their storage limits.

When viewing a message listing, you can click the checkbox located next to each message and then move the checked messages to the savebox or delete them by using the appropriate action button at the bottom of the listing. Be careful not to confuse the Delete All button with Delete Marked; even though they both look the same (even the Are you sure... confirmation message), Delete All clears *all* the contents of a PM box.

Time For Action—The Dude PMs the Administrator

1. You're logged in as The Dude. Click the You have no new messages
   @ You have no new messages link at the top navigation menu. You're now in your empty and lonely inbox.

2. Click New Post. You're presented with the interface for writing a PM; this interface is similar to the one for writing a posting.

3. You want to PM the Administrator user, the user you created during installation as described in Chapter 2. Suppose you're not sure if it was called Administrator or simply Admin. Click the Find a username button next to the text field for the username of the recipient. A new window shows up.

4. Type Admin* (note the asterisk) and click Search (* is a wildcard, which means *any username* starting with "Admin" should be matched.

5. A dropdown with the matches appears; in our case, there's only one match. Click Select.

6. Now the username field is pre-filled. Enter test #1 in the subject line and the same in the message body. Add :) to make it friendlier.
7. Click Preview. Looks good?
8. Click Submit to send the message.
9. Repeat the steps with test #2 as a subject line and a message body.
10. Go to your sentbox. It's empty.
11. Go to your outbox. You see the two messages that you've just sent. Check the box next to test #1.
12. Click Delete Marked and confirm the deletion.
13. Log out, and log back in as Administrator. Go to your inbox by using the You have 1 new message link.
14. You see that you have a new PM from The Dude with the subject test #2. Click the subject line to read the message.
15. Click Save Message to move the message to the savebox.

What Just Happened?

You've successfully created, sent, altered, received, and saved a PM. If you now log back in as The Dude, you'll see that your outbox is empty, but the sentbox now contains the test #2 message.

Voting in Polls

You already know that polls can be created when posting a new topic. Here are some notes about voting in these polls:

- Only registered users can vote.
- Non-registered users only see the poll results.
- The votes are kept confidential; there's no way to tell how a particular user has voted.
- You can view the results without voting by selecting View Results.
- Don't forget that the poll results are not 100% reliable, because an existing user can register as a new member only to vote a second time.

Staying Current with the Topics

As you know already, you can get a notification if someone posts a reply to a topic that you created or posted in. You can **subscribe** to this topic by making sure Notify me when a reply is posted is checked when you write your posting. In addition to that, you can start watching a topic even if you don't post in it. You can do so by using the Watch this topic for replies link located at the bottom of the topic. You can stop receiving notifications on a topic's update at any time, by using the Stop watching this topic link at the bottom of every page of the topic you're watching.

Viewing Information about Other Users

There are a few ways to find about the other members of the community. The memberlist feature and the usergroups provide different sorts of user listings, while the "Who's online" feature provides information about who is currently logged in and what are they currently doing.

Memberlist

If users want to know more about the other members of the community, they can obtain a member listing. Clicking the Memberlist top navigation link will bring up a list of all registered users. There are sorting options at the top of this listing. If, for example, you want to get a spicier listing like "Hmm, who's posting the most?", you can sort on the basis of the number of posts. You can select Total posts as Select sort method and Descending as your Order. This will show you the top posting members.

Well, in our example board, there's nothing spicy in the list of just the Administrator and The Dude, but it can get much more interesting as your community grows. Here's how this type of Memberlist report looks like when executed on phpBB.com's community:

phpBB.com Forum Index			Select sort method: Total posts	Order Descending		Sort
#		Username	E-mail	Location	Joined	Posts	Website
1	88 pm	A_Jelly_Doughnut		Jesusland!	17 Jan 2003	24869	www
2	88 pm	primedomain		Bavaria	15 Dec 2001	23513	www
3	88 pm	Techie-Micheal			13 Oct 2001	16832	
4	88 pm	zeroK		Klagenfurt / Austria	20 Jan 2002	16369	www
5	88 pm	ZoliveR		I'm floating down, ready to bite and eat you !	14 Jul 2002	15353	www
6	88 pm	flogger12	email		24 Nov 2003	9751	
7	88 pm	psoTFX			03 Jul 2001	9251	

Usergroups

This is an advanced phpBB feature that allows the creation of groups of users based on some criteria. Groups are defined by an administrator and are assigned a group moderator. By default, no groups exist. Users can apply to join a usergroup, and depending on the configuration (there might or might not be a need for the group moderator to approve the users), are approved.

Who Is Online

This section of the board homepage was already mentioned. Interestingly, there is a sort of a hidden feature here—something that is not obvious enough for most people to notice. It's the fact that the Who is Online heading is actually a link. (The same is true for the title of a forum category.)

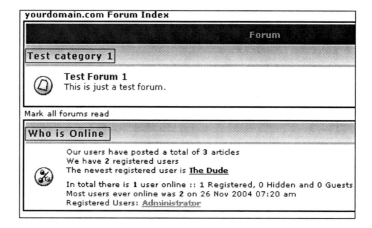

Clicking Who is Online will bring a special "spy" screen, which is publicly available. This sneaky feature allows everybody to see what others are doing at the moment.

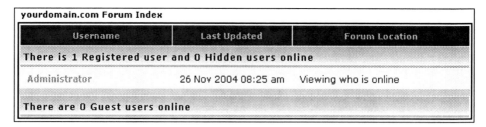

This can potentially become a long list of all currently logged-in users as well as the guests currently browsing the site.

4
User Experience: Moderators and Administrators

In the previous chapter you saw how phpBB works from a visitor's perspective.

In this chapter you will see the moderators' and administrators' side of the coin. You will learn:

- What the moderator's capabilities are
- How the most popular administration features work

Moderator Experience

At this point you have a pretty good idea about the regular members' perspective of your board. Now let's look at how a moderator works with phpBB. To begin with, what *is* a moderator? All dictionary definitions aside, a moderator is a community member who has some more privileges over the postings and the topics than those that the regular users have. Moderators are usually respected veteran members who are volunteering their time and energy to make the forum a better place for discussions in line with the administrator's vision for the community.Moderators are your best helpers in managing your site, so you should make sure you make their tasks clear to them and educate them so that they don't have any technical difficulties on the way.

In order to visualize better what's discussed in the chapter, you need a moderator account. You can make our The Dude user a moderator, or you can create a new user and assign moderator privileges to it. Let's take The Dude as an example.

Time For Action—Assigning Moderator Privileges to a User

1. Log in as an administrator.
2. Go to the Administration Panel.
3. In the left-hand menu, under User Admin click on the Permissions link.

4. You are now in the User Permissions Control section.
5. In the textbox, type in The Dude and click Look Up User.

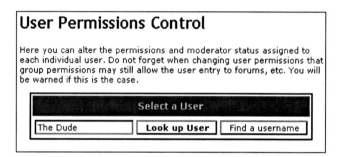

6. Now you see a form to set the permissions for The Dude.
7. Select Is Moderator as shown in the illustration and click Submit:

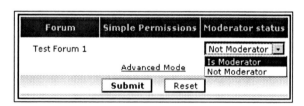

What Just Happened?

You've successfully changed The Dude's authorization level; this user is now a moderator for Test Forum 1. Log out from your administrator account and log back in as The Dude, and you're ready to start exploring what a moderator can do.

A moderator can take up two groups of tasks; these are related to *managing postings* and *managing topics*.

Managing Postings

Now that you're logged in as The Dude, the moderator, if you go to any posting and look at the actions area for the posting, you'll see the buttons for all actions a moderator can perform on a posting.

Editing and Deleting

Editing posts and deleting them from the users' perspective was already discussed earlier in this chapter. It's the same thing for moderators with only one simple but quite significant difference: in the default phpBB configuration, moderators can edit and delete *any* posting for the topic, and not just *their* postings.

Editing the First Posting in a Topic

When a moderator edits the first posting in a discussion, there are some more options, because the first post contains some topic-related information. For example, changing the post's subject changes the topic's subject.

There are also options for changing the type of the posting/topic. The possible options for the topic type are as shown:

If you post a topic as Announcement or Sticky, it will stay on the top of the topic listings. One difference between the two types is in the icon that will be displayed next to the topic title. Another (more important) difference is that sticky topics are displayed on the top of the first page of topic listings, while the announcements are on the top of all listing pages. What this means is that if there are so many topics in your forum that they span several pages (a page has 25 topics by default), a topic marked Announcement will be on top of *all the pages*, whereas the Stickys will be on the top of the *first page only*. Here's an example of what a sticky topic and an announcement look like.

(🗎 new topic)	yourdomain.com Forum Index -> Test Forum 1			Mark all topics read
Topics	**Replies**	**Author**	**Views**	**Last Post**
ⓘ Announcement: Great news!	0	The Dude	29	Fri Nov 26, 2004 7:47 am The Dude ➔🗋
⚄ Sticky: An important topic - terms of using the forum	0	The Dude	1	Sun Nov 28, 2004 3:27 am The Dude ➔🗋
ⓐ Just a good old normal topic	0	The Dude	1	Sun Nov 28, 2004 3:28 am The Dude ➔🗋
ⓐ Welcome to phpBB 2	0	Administrator	7	Sat Oct 21, 2000 12:01 am Administrator ➔🗋

Display topics from previous: [All Topics ▼] [Go]

Another specific thing about editing the first posting in a topic is that you have the option of deleting it in the edit interface.

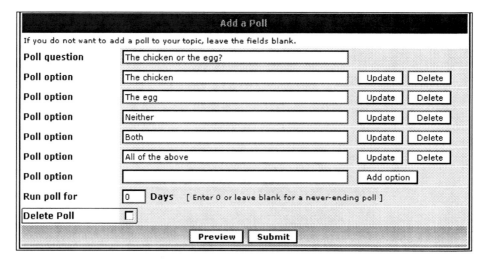

If a posting contains a poll, the poll can also be edited or deleted.

Here are some other specifics about editing the first post in a topic. It's a good idea to try the listed scenarios yourself, just to make sure you feel comfortable doing it.

- If it's the only posting in the topic and you delete it, the topic is deleted.
- If the first posting contains a poll and you delete the posting, the poll stays.
- If there are other postings after the first when you delete it, the topic stays. The title of the topic is kept from the deleted post subject.
- A poll can be safely removed from a topic, keeping everything else as is.

Viewing Poster's IP Address

If you click the IP action icon, you are presented with the IP information screen.

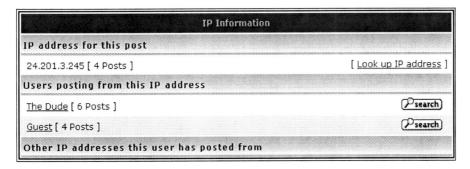

What you see on this screen is the IP address of the user, a list of users that have posted using this IP address, and finally a list of other IP addresses (if any) that were used by this user to post other messages. Here is some information that you might find useful:

- An IP address is a numeric identifier, unique for every computer connected to the Internet. IP stands for Internet Protocol. Internet Service Providers (ISP) all over the world assign IP addresses to their clients every time an Internet connection is requested. This means that if you connect to the Internet, disconnect, and reconnect, the IP address assigned to you the second time may be different from that assigned the first time.

- If you click the Look up IP address link shown in the above screenshot, phpBB will try to resolve (give a friendlier representation of) the IP address. This feature may not always work, because not all IP addresses can be resolved. In the example above, the numeric IP address will be resolved as shown in the image below:

IP Information	
IP address for this post	
modemcable245.3-201-24.mc.videotron.ca [4 Posts]	[Look up IP address]
Users posting from this IP address	
The Dude [6 Posts]	search
Guest [4 Posts]	search
Other IP addresses this user has posted from	

The last part of the IP address (videotron.ca) gives information about the Internet Service Provider (ISP). Some companies have their own IP addresses, and they act as if they were their own ISP. Resolving a poster's IP address can at times give you information about the poster's employer or the poster's ISP, or no information if it cannot be resolved. Keep in mind:

- One user can be listed with several IP addresses, and this can happen quite often, because ISPs change the IP addresses assigned to their clients. Also, a member can use more than one computer and Internet connection to post (for example, home and office computers).

- Several users may use the same IP address. Maybe the first possibility you think of is that a person has registered a new username and is posting from both usernames. Although it's a probable scenario, it's not necessarily always the case. Two users may have the same ISP (or may be employed at the same company) and thus may have the same IP address. Another explanation is that two users are friends and one is using the other's computer and Internet connection to post. And yet another—two users are posting from the same Internet club (game club, Internet café, etc.).

- In the IP information interface, clicking on the username brings up the user's profile page.

- In the same interface, clicking on the Search button will list all posts by a particular user.

Managing Topics

Managing topics is the second group of options that a moderator has that the regular users don't. One way to manage a topic is by altering the first posting in this topic. This was discussed in the *Managing Postings* section earlier in this chapter (you might want to go back and take a look; the other options discussed here are strictly topics-related).

At the bottom of every topic, a moderator has access to four action icons, as shown:

In the order that they appear, they mean:

- **Delete a topic**: Remove the topic permanently from the database.
- **Move a topic**: Move the topic from its present forum to another forum. Another forum refers to a forum in the same bulletin board.
- **Lock a topic**: Users (except moderators and administrators) can no longer post in this topic.
- **Split a topic**: Divide a topic into two.

Deleting, Locking, and Unlocking Topics

All these options are actually simple to use. You just need to list a topic and then select the appropriate action icon. phpBB then asks you to confirm the chosen action. That's it! The unlock icon ⚽ is displayed only in locked topics.

Moving Topics

In order to test this functionality, you need at least two forums. So before you continue, let's first create a new forum.

Time For Action—Creating a Forum

1. Log in as Administrator (the user account you created when installing), and then click the Go to Administration Panel link.

2. On the left-hand menu, under Forum Admin, click Management.

3. Type New Forum in the first field, and click on Create new forum.

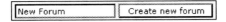

4. You see a new form; leave it as is and click Create new forum.

5. Go back to the forum, clicking the phpBB icon on the top left.

What Just Happened?

You've created a new forum. Don't worry about the details; they will be discussed in more detail later in this chapter. OK, back to moving topics. This simply involves displacing a topic to another forum, and is often needed when somebody posts a topic in not-the-best-place on the bulletin board. Log out now and log back in as The Dude.

A moderator moves a topic by selecting the ⊘ action icon. The following confirmation screen is displayed:

This screen lets the moderator select the forum to which the topic is to be moved. There is also a Leave shadow topic in old forum checkbox (checked by default). Select this option to leave in the old forum a link to the new location. The link looks exactly like a normal topic, except that it has Moved before the title, as shown here:

Splitting Topics

Sometimes a discussion digresses from the original topic; at other times, people discuss two different questions in the same topic—postings start overlapping, and it's difficult to follow the discussion. To avoid confusion caused by such a situation, a moderator can split the discussion into two topics. To do so, the moderator clicks the split icon ⓐ. The following special interface for splitting topics is presented:

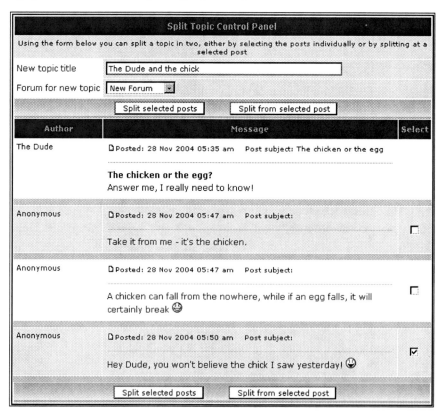

Essentially, splitting a topic involves creating a new topic to accommodate some already existing messages, while removing them from the topic under which they were originally posted. Thus said, a new topic needs a title, a forum to reside in, and at least one posting.

The Split Topic Control Panel shows a text field for the title and a dropdown to choose an existing forum. There is a checkbox next to each posting. There are two splitting options:

- To select each posting individually. It's time-consuming to check each individual posting, but this is an option when two separate questions are discussed in a total overlap.

- To select one posting and then split the complete discussion. This is applicable when at some point a discussion takes a totally different direction. In this case, the checked posting is the beginning of the *new* topic.

Two tips

Especially on heavily loaded boards, it's a good idea to temporarily lock a topic before splitting. This gives enough time for the moderator to rethink the details, while preventing other users from posting at the same time and adding to the confusion.

Have in mind that the author of the first message in the newly created topic becomes the author of the new topic.

Doing It All Together—The Moderator Control Panel

phpBB has a feature called the Moderator Control Panel, which gives access to all the actions discussed above for managing topics. To access this interface, click the moderate this forum link, located at the bottom-right corner of every forum page.

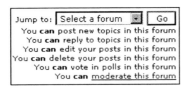

This brings up the Moderator Control Panel interface (screenshot overleaf):

- This interface has a Select checkbox next to each topic, and a number of action buttons at the bottom. It allows you to check several topics and perform an action on all of them at once.

- Clicking a topic title brings up the Split Topic interface.

- All actions (deleting, locking, unlocking, moving, and splitting) work in the exact same way as already discussed earlier in this chapter, only the interface is different so as to allow altering multiple topics at once.

The following screenshot shows the Moderator Control Panel:

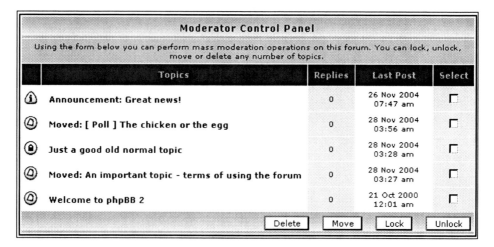

Administrator Experience

This is it. You've come to the most important part—administering your board. You've already seen some of the features described previously in this chapter as well as in Chapter 2, but it's now time to take a more organized approach and make sure you understand what your administrative options are and how to use them.

This section will later describe some basic phpBB admin features that you're likely to use more frequently than others. For more advanced and exotic options, make sure you read Chapter 6, which goes into details about security-related questions, smilies, usergroups, and other issues.

In order to test what's being described further on, you need to log in as a user with administrative privileges. There can be multiple administrators to your board, but in any event, at least one administrative user account exists—the account created while installing phpBB. Well, log in with this account, use the Go to Administration Panel link, and let's start exploring administrative options.

Administration Panel Overview

The Administration Panel has two main areas (referred to as **frames** in HTML terms):

- The left-hand navigation area, which contains links to all your administrative options. It's divided into groups of similar options like Forum Admin, User Admin, etc.
- The right-hand content area, where the appropriate content is loaded when you click a link from the navigation area.

Your Administration Panel front page looks as shown on the following screenshot:

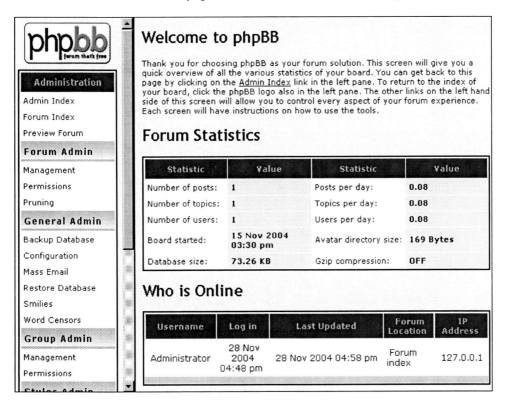

The Administration Panel front page also has some general statistics about the forum usage, and a Who is Online section that works in a similar way to the one that visitors can access on the forum homepage (see the *Visitor Experience* section earlier in the chapter), except that this one has an IP address column as well. Clicking on an IP address redirects you to a third-party site that provides some IP-related tools that you may find useful.

The first three options of the navigation menu are pretty straightforward and you may want to give them a try just to get a more comfortable feeling browsing the Administration Panel. They are not actually administrative options but are simply links to the board's front page and the Administration Panel. The phpBB logo in the top-left corner is also a link to the homepage of the board.

Now let's take a closer look at the other groups of options on the navigation menu.

Forum Admin

As the title says, this is a group of options for you to administer your forums, to create, edit, delete, or rearrange forums and their categories, as well as to set their options and rules of use (referred to as **permissions**).

Forum Management

Clicking the Management link in the Forum Admin options group brings up the Forum Administration interface. This interface allows you to create, edit, and delete forums and to organize them into categories.

Creating New Forums and Categories

The simplest way to create a new forum was already briefly discussed in the *Moderator Experience* section. Now let's take a more detailed approach. The following screenshot shows how the interface looks after we've added the new forum in the previous section. If you haven't done what was described in the *Moderator Experience* section, you'll have the default phpBB look, which is same as shown below minus the New Forum row:

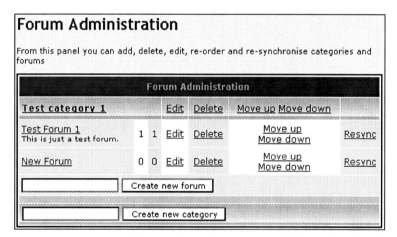

Time For Action—Creating a New Category

1. Type Fun in the second text field of the Forum Administration interface.

2. Click Create new category.

3. Click the link in the Click Here to return to Forum Administration line once the category is created.

What Just Happened

You've created a new blank category (blank because it doesn't contain any forums yet). Here's how the Forum Administration screen will look after you complete the earlier steps:

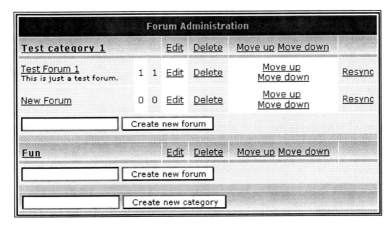

At this point, because the new category is still empty, visitors see no changes made to the board's homepage.

Now let's add some forums to the new category.

Time For Action—Creating a New Forum

1. Type Funny pics in the textbox after the Fun category you've just added in the Forum Administration interface.

2. Click Create new forum. You are now presented with the following form:

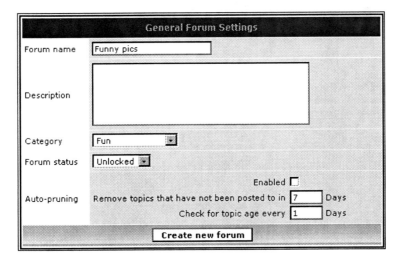

3. In the Description field, type Collection of links to funny images found on the web.

4. Leave Category dropdown as is.

5. Leave the Forum status dropdown as is.

6. In the Auto-pruning section, leave the defaults.

7. Click the Create new forum button.

8. Click the link Click Here to return to Forum Administration. At this point we are repeating the exercise, but with a few modifications.

9. To start creating another new forum, type Funny quotes, but this time do it in the *first* text field.

10. In the Description field, type Here you'll find links to funny quote web sites the admin finds amusing.

11. Change the value in the Category dropdown from Test category 1 to Fun.

12. Change the value in the Forum status dropdown from Unlocked to Locked.

13. In the Auto-pruning section, select Enabled.

14. In the Auto-pruning section, change the first text value from 7 to 30.

15. In the Auto-pruning section, change the second text value from 1 to 7.

16. Click the Create new forum button.

17. Click the link in the Click Here to return to Forum Administration.

What Just Happened

Here's the result of what you've just done as shown in the Administration Panel:

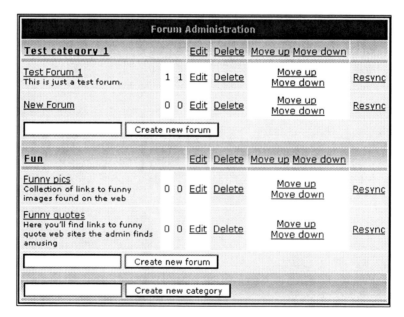

And here's what your users will see—the changed board on the home page:

Forum	Topics	Posts	Last Post
Test category 1			
Test Forum 1 This is just a test forum.	1	1	21 Oct 2000 12:01 am Administrator ➡️
New Forum	0	0	No Posts
Fun			
Funny pics Collection of links to funny images found on the web	0	0	No Posts
Funny quotes Here you'll find links to funny quote web sites the admin finds amusing	0	0	No Posts

Now let's take a step back and see exactly what happened, using the same numbers as in the preceding *Time For Action* section:

1. You gave a name to your new forum.
2. You initiated the creation of the new forum.
3. You gave a description to your forum.
4. You used the phpBB-proposed value for a category.
5. You used the phpBB-proposed value for the Locked/Unlocked forum status (in this case, Unlocked). What this means is that users can post in this forum. Locked, as you know, would mean that users cannot post in the forum, but administrators and moderators still can.
6. You used the phpBB default value for the Auto-pruning option, which is to *not* use this option. If you enable the auto-pruning feature, phpBB will delete all topics that were inactive for a specified period of time. The Inactivity of a topic is counted from the time of the last posting to it.
7. You finalized the creation of the new forum.
8. You went back to the Forums Administration interface.
9. You started the process of creating a new forum again and set the title.
10. You specified the forum description.
11. This time you didn't use the proposed value, but changed the forum category. This category was proposed by phpBB, because you typed the forum name under Test category 1 and not under Fun on step 9.

12. You decided to have this forum locked so that users would not able to post, but you still could.

13. You turned on the auto-pruning option.

14. You set that phpBB should delete all topics older than 30 days, counted from the date of the last posting in this topic.

15. You set phpBB to check topics for auto-deletion every seven days.

16. You finalized the creation of the new forum.

17. You went back to the Forums Administration interface.

Fine Tuning Existing Forums and Categories

After a forum is created, it can be managed further—edited, deleted, or positioned in relation to the other forums in the board.

Editing

You can edit an existing category or a forum by clicking the Edit link located next to the title of the category or forum. The edit forms look exactly the same as the forms for Create new forum and work the same way.

Deleting

You can delete categories and forums by using the Delete links next to their titles. One specific point here: when you delete a forum or a category that has been around for some time and people have been posting in it, you might not want to delete *all* the postings. To simplify this, phpBB allows you to move the existing topics into another forum or a category before deleting the selected topic.

When you delete a category, you can pick a new category to move all forums to, as shown below (this interface shows Delete Forum and Forum name, but actually refers to deleting categories; you'll spot the difference with the actual deleting-a-forum interface):

When you want to delete a forum, you are given the option of moving all the topics to another forum. Unlike with category deletion, when you delete a forum you can even choose to delete the topics and the postings as well. Think again before using this option though. Deleting your community's postings may not be such a good idea.

Changing Display Order

You can change the order of displaying categories and forums on the board's home page, by using the Move up and Move down links, next to each forum or a category.

Time For Action—Tweaking Display Order

1. Click the Move down link next to the Test category 1 category.
2. Click the Move up link next to the New Forum forum.

What Just Happened

The Fun category is now the first one that the users will see. Also, within Test Category 1, you've switched the forums' order so that New Forum is displayed before Test Forum 1. Here's how users will see your board after the tweaks:

Forum	Topics	Posts	Last Post
Fun			
Funny pics Collection of links to funny images found on the web	0	0	No Posts
Funny quotes Here you'll find links to funny quote web sites the admin finds amusing	0	0	No Posts
Test category 1			
New Forum	0	0	No Posts
Test Forum 1 This is just a test forum.	1	1	21 Oct 2000 12:01 am Administrator

Using the Resync Options

If you spot some weird things happening on you board, use the Resync option as a first attempt at recovery. If there are some data inconsistencies for whatever reasons, Resync will try to bring the data into a consistent state.

Resync can do no harm to the board data. So don't worry, you can't break anything. (Well, don't take that last sentence as a challenge.) If ever in doubt about whether you should be using this option, just use it. On the other hand, if you find yourself using it too often, there might be other problems; isolate the symptoms and seek a cure on the phpBB community forums.

Who Can Do What—Setting Up Forum Permissions

phpBB takes the security aspects of running a bulletin board really seriously. That's why there is a powerful and options-rich system of permissions and user privileges. You'll find some more detailed information about the permissions system in Chapter 6, which contains details on some advanced phpBB features. You'll also find more information in the online phpBB user guide. So before you start playing around with the permissions, make sure you know what you're doing. For now, we'll just take a quick look into the permissions that are used most often, and leave the details for later.

There are two modes of setting a forum's permissions: **simple** and **advanced**. Using the simple mode, you can pick permission patterns (a set of advanced permissions grouped together to be easier to use) from a list of preset values. Example options for simple mode are "Public" forum, "Registered" forum, and "Hidden" forum.

These simple options are carefully analyzed and selected by the phpBB team, so using them instead of the advanced options is probably the safest thing to do until you are comfortable managing forum and user permissions. Let this be your rule of thumb: use the simple mode unless you have a good reason not to and you know what you're doing.

The two simple mode options used the most frequently are "Registered" and "Public". To get a rough idea, in a "Public" forum, a visitor doesn't have to be a registered user in order to post. In a "Registered" forum, only registered users can post. In both cases, only moderators and administrators can use more advanced features like specifying topic-type (sticky and announcement) or editing and deleting other people's posts.

By default, all the forums that phpBB creates are public. A good (and common) practice is to change a forum's permissions to "Registered" after you create it.

Time For Action—Setting Forum Permissions in Simple Mode

1. Select Permissions from the Forum Admin options in the left navigation:

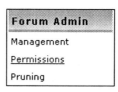

2. Select the Funny pics forum and click on the Look up Forum button.
3. Select Registered from the Simple Mode options dropdown and click Submit.

What Just Happened?

Only registered users are now allowed to post in the "Funny pics" forum. You did this by setting phpBB permissions in simple mode.

Pruning

Pruning is a feature that allows you to clean up old inactive topics to free up database space. You already saw how the auto-pruning feature works. The only way pruning is different from auto-pruning is that it's initiated by you, and not done automatically.

Think twice before you use this feature—deleting topics is irreversible! Are you sure you don't need these topics anymore? Remember that your community members have spent quite some time writing all these postings. Do you want to throw their postings away? Consider buying more database space if you're short, before deleting people's topics. If you're still positive you want to prune postings, here's how.

Time For Action—Pruning a Forum

1. Select Pruning from the Forum Admin options from the left navigation menu.

2. Pick All forums if you want to clean them all. You also have the option of pruning individual forums.
3. Type 30 as the number of days.
4. Click Do Prune.

What Just Happened?

You've just deleted all topics in all forums that were inactive for more than 30 days. Here's a sample outcome of this action; this is a report of how many topics and postings were deleted:

Forum Prune

Pruning of forums was successful

Forum	Topics pruned	Posts pruned
Funny pics	0	0
Funny quotes	0	0
New Forum	0	0
Test Forum 1	1	1

Systems Administration Using General Admin Options

Now let's move to the General Admin group of options, which allow you to do the basic system administration tasks.

Configuration

You can access the general configuration options by clicking the Configuration link from the General Admin options on the left navigation menu. (Don't worry about skipping Backup Database; a description of this option follows in a bit.)

This brings the "General Configuration" form that contains the very root board settings, such as domain name, enabling private messages, and so on. You already know about these settings from Chapter 2.

Database Backup and Restore

It's a good idea to make backup copies of your data, just in case something happens. Your hosting provider is likely to make such backup copies; you can also make backups using phpMyAdmin or using MySQL command-line utilities. If you're using a different database system, you may have other options. If you have access to phpMyAdmin, use it. If your hosting provider is making copies, find out about their frequency and the level of effort required to restore the database. It's your responsibility not to allow data to be lost, and it should be taken seriously.

Scared ya, huh? Good. Now for the good news: if you're worried you don't have access to tools to back up your data, rest assured, phpBB provides you with a database backup utility. Sometimes it can be your only option, so let's look into it.

Time For Action—Backing Up Your Board Data

1. Click Backup Database from the navigation menu.
2. In the Backup Options form that you see, click Start Backup, leaving all values at default. You get a Please wait message.
3. A file dialog window asks you what to do with the phpbb_db_backup.sql file that was requested for download. Save this file into a selected folder on your computer.

What Just Happened

You've just created a backup file containing the SQL instructions for your database and saved it on your computer. It's a good idea to store these backup files carefully, keeping them organized by using appropriate filenames and directories. For example, filenames can contain the date the backup was created. Every once in a while, burn those files on a CD; you never know when your PC will crash and cause you to lose your data backups.

Time For Action—Restoring Your Database from a Backup Copy

1. Click Restore Database from the left navigation menu in the Administration Panel.
2. Locate an existing backup copy file (you can use the `phpbb_db_backup.sql` file you created in the previous exercise).
3. Click Start Restore.
4. If everything is OK, you'll get a message that the restore was successful.

What Just Happened

You restored your board database from a backup copy saved on your computer, containing all configuration, forums, topics, users: to put it simply—all the data your board needs in order to run.

Depending on the size of the database, the time taken to execute backup and restore operations may vary. For very large databases, these operations may even fail because of some server restrictions imposed by your hosting provider. If you're experiencing problems, be sure to read Chapter 6 for more information on database backup and restore options, and feel free to seek advice on phpBB.com or phpBBHacks.com forums.

Mass Email

You can use phpBB to send an email to all your users, or to just one usergroup. This feature is really easy to use: you just select the Mass Email link from the menu on the left, select the recipients, type in the subject and the message body, and click the E-mail button. This hopefully will fire an email to all users. "Hopefully", because there is a chance that this feature will not work for you. Because of all these people that send unsolicited mail (read **spam**), Internet providers and hosting companies are taking measures against everything that looks like a mass mail. So if you have a lot of users in your database or your host has strict mail-usage rules, you may not be able to mass-mail your users.

You can try using the SMTP server of your ISP if the attempt to send without any configuration changes fails. The mail settings are located under the Configuration link in the General Admin section.

The way phpBB mailer works is it adds all recipients to the BCC. Imagine you're sending a normal email in your favorite email environment. Now imagine you add all users in the BCC (Blind Carbon Copy) field. The result: the email is sent to all recipients, and they cannot see who else is on the BCC list.

Smilies

You know smilies, those cute little icons (also known as emoticons) that you can use to lighten up your postings and show some emotion, as well as to give the reader a cue as to how to react to your text. Well, good news: phpBB comes with a package of smilies by default and is also flexible enough to allow you to add, edit, and delete the smilies that your members can use in their postings.

Clicking Smilies in the General Admin option group brings the Smiles Editing Utility.

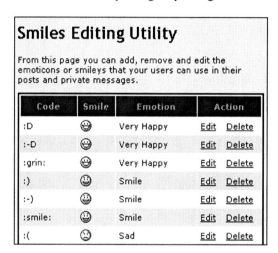

It's pretty easy to edit or delete smilies. Just use the corresponding link located next to each smilie. You can also add new icons and even add batches of new icons, packaged in special files (.pak). There's more information on this in Chapter 6.

Filtering Words Using Word Censors

phpBB allows you to censor words that your members use in their postings. Censoring means replacing a bad word with another (not as bad) one. It actually doesn't need to be a word per se; it can be a part of a word or a phrase.

Time For Action—Creating a Word Filter

1. Click on the Word Censors link on the navigation menu.
2. In the new screen, click Add new word. A new form appears:

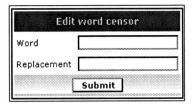

3. Type The Dude Sucks in the Word field.
4. Type The Dude Rocks! in the Replacement field.
5. Click Submit.

What Just Happened

You introduced a new word replacement filter for posting texts. You can now go to the board's front end and test how this feature works.

Some additional information:

- The words you choose to censor will be censored not only in posting texts but also in post/topic subjects, PM, usernames, polls answers, and poll questions.

- The words are replaced only when displaying. In the database, phpBB stores the original texts. So if you decide to remove a word censor, the original text will start showing up.

- You can use the * wildcard to match a partial word. In the previous example, if you go with matching and replacing The Dude su*, this will also match all alternative phrases like The Dude sukz, The Dude sux, etc., and all of them will be replaced.

Introduction to User Management

Managing users is an activity that you might do quite often. Sometimes users have problems with their profiles, forget passwords, no longer have access to old email accounts, and so on. This is when you step in to help your users.

This section, as the title says, is an introduction and contains only the features you are likely to use more or less frequently. More advanced and less used features will be discussed in Chapter 6.

Editing User Profiles

To edit a user profile, click on the Management link of the User Admin options.

You are already familiar with the screen for selecting a user based on the username. If you're not sure about a username spelling, use the Find a username feature.

After you type (or find) a username, clicking the Look up user button brings up the user profile. The form for editing the profile is the same as the one the users see on the board front end with one addition: the Special admin-only fields section:

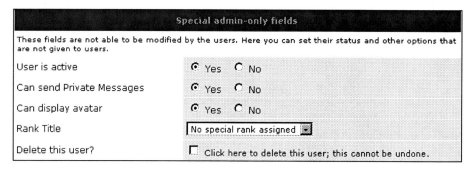

The options are quite self-explanatory:

- You can deactivate the user, so the user can no longer log in.
- You can disallow the use of private messaging or avatars for this user. Disallowing PM means that the user cannot send a PM, but can receive PMs from other users.
- You can assign a rank (ranks and avatars are discussed further).
- You can delete this user.

Deleting Users

To delete a user, follow the steps described in the previous section, check the Delete this user? checkbox at the bottom of the edit form, and click Submit. Deleting a user is permanent; and cannot be reverted. However, deleting a user doesn't mean deleting all the postings made by the user. When a user is deleted, all the postings by this user become "guest" postings. At this point, the username is recycled and becomes available for a new registration.

Permissions

The interface for setting user permissions can be accessed using the Permissions link in the User Admin navigation group:

Again you are presented with the familiar Select a User form. After choosing the user to edit, you see the User Permissions Control screen:

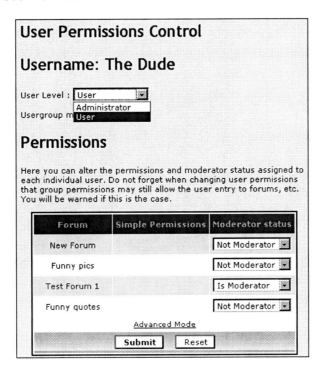

Here, you have the option of making this user an administrator, which will automatically give the user access to the Administration Panel and will make the user a moderator of all the forums. In short, this means that the user will have exactly the same privileges as you.

The other option is to selectively make the user a moderator on per-forum basis. You've already done this; remember how you made The Dude a moderator at the beginning of the *Moderator Experience* section?

Here the Simple Permissions column is empty. The same is true for the detailed permissions of you click on Advanced mode. This is because these options are applicable and can be set for private forums only, and there's no private forum among those listed. Private forums and detailed permissions are described further in the book.

Banning Users

Yes, it's not a pleasant task, throwing out users. But what can you do? C'est la vie, it happens. There are all kinds of people out there, and sometimes hidden behind the anonymity of the Web, some folks start doing things that they wouldn't normally do. Like using bad grammar. Or forgetting to post on Thursdays. Just joking, of course.

Anyway, the idea is that it's up to you to define unwanted behavior for your specific community, but when it comes to the worst, you'd better know what your options are.

To access the ban control interface, use the Ban Control link under User Admin from the navigation menu on the left-hand side.

The interface for banning users may seem a bit confusing at first, but it's actually good for providing an at-a-glance overview of what sort of bans are currently defined. The form consists of three groups of two form fields each. These three groups represent the three ways to ban a user, and the two fields are for adding and removing bans respectively. The form itself contains some help on the available options.

Ban one or more specific users	
Username:	[ ] Find a username

Un-ban one more specific users	
Username: You can unban multiple users in one go using the appropriate combination of mouse and keyboard for your computer and browser	The Dude ▲ ▼

Ban one or more IP addresses or hostnames	
IP addresses or hostnames: To specify several different IP addresses or hostnames separate them with commas. To specify a range of IP addresses, separate the start and end with a hyphen (-); to specify a wildcard, use an asterisk (*).	[ ]

Un-ban one or more IP addresses	
IP addresses or hostnames: You can unban multiple IP addresses in one go using the appropriate combination of mouse and keyboard for your computer and browser	123.123.123.123 ▲ ▼

Ban one or more email addresses	
E-mail address: To specify more than one email address, separate them with commas. To specify a wildcard username, use * like *@hotmail.com	[ ]

Un-ban one or more email addresses	
E-mail address: You can unban multiple email addresses in one go using the appropriate combination of mouse and keyboard for your computer and browser	bad.guy@scary-host.com ▲ ▼

When you ban a user using any of the three methods and the user tries to access the forum, he or she will see a message as follows:

Critical Information
You have been banned from this forum. Please contact the webmaster or board administrator for more information.

Disallowing Users

While you can ban users after the damage is done, disallowing certain usernames is a preventative act. When a username (or a part of it) is disallowed, it cannot be used for registrations. So this feature is used before a username is taken, to prevent it from being taken. The form for disallowing usernames contains an interface for both adding and removing rules. The form is accessible through the Disallow names link on the left.

The following example shows how everything starting with Mod (as in Moderator) or Admin is disallowed to prevent imposters from using usernames suggesting that they are not just regular users, but have special community powers.

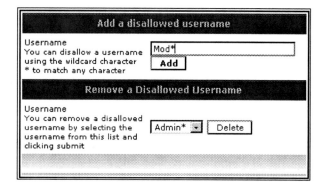

Summary

Running through the phpBB's basic features was a long way to go. This is true, because phpBB is a feature-rich bulletin-board system that provides a lot of flexibility to all user types—regular members, moderators, and administrators. To get philosophical, in theory and practice, it is known that greater flexibility often comes at the price of increased complexity. But this is not necessarily the case for most of the phpBB features as they are really intuitive and easy to use.

If you did the *Time For Action* sections in this chapter, you should now have a pretty good idea how things are working around your new BB. If you didn't do the practice parts, now is the time to go back and do them or just to set the book aside and jump into experimenting with phpBB, you favorite bulletin-board system.

5

Customizing Your Forum

Now that you have installed phpBB and gained some experience with the Administration Control Panel, you are ready to begin altering some more advanced aspects of the forum's appearance and features. Changing these areas of phpBB will be essential for giving your forum a unique identity that stands out among online forums. The appearance of a forum is mainly controlled by phpBB's styling system, which manages the colors, images, and visual layout of the forum. Features can be added, removed, or altered by installing modification scripts downloaded from phpBB-related websites.

By the end of this chapter, you will have learned about:

- The basics of a phpBB 2.0 style
- Correct methods of editing phpBB files
- How to add and remove styles
- Common style installation problems
- Ways to customize a style
- The benefits of creating and altering styles
- Methods of changing forum images
- How to add new forum features

phpBB Styles

If you look at several different phpBB forums, you may notice several differences in each forum. They may use different colors and images, display features in a different order, or omit some features entirely. This multitude of effects can be accomplished by using different phpBB styles. A phpBB **style** is the appearance of a forum, created by a combination of a layout, colors, and images. When you installed phpBB, the default style, called subSilver, was also installed. subSilver is the most commonly used style on phpBB forums, but there are well over two hundred different styles that have been publicly released. It is common for forums to have multiple styles available for user selection.

> When dealing with phpBB, you will sometimes see the terms style, theme, and template used interchangeably. In this chapter, themes and templates are defined as two smaller aspects of the overall style to reduce confusion. This is the way the terms are used most often in phpBB's code and Administration Control Panel. Even the latter sometimes uses theme in place of style, however.

Structure of a Style

In order to effectively customize a style, you must first understand the parts that compose the design of that style. Styles, like houses, are built from smaller components that work together to create a frame. That frame, like the walls of the house, provides a structure for displaying the internal contents of a forum. These frames can be very complex creations so let us look at how the basic pieces are put together and stored, before we get into the actual customization of a style.

Style Elements

Styles are composed of three primary **style elements**, or smaller portions that work together to create the overall visual appearance of the style. These are the template, theme, and image set elements. Each style is self-contained and includes all the style elements needed to operate correctly.

The first and most important part of a style is the template element. The **template element** is a set of text files containing the entire markup that is used to generate the visual layout of a forum. The **markup** consists mainly of a markup language such as **Hypertext Markup Language (HTML)** and phpBB's own special template features, but can also include client-side scripting languages such as JavaScript. Template files are used to arrange most of the information displayed by your forum. You can identify template files by looking at the name of a file; all template files have names ending with tpl. Some examples are index_body.tpl, viewtopic_body.tpl, and message_body.tpl. Although this is rare, it is possible for multiple styles to use one set of template files with different themes and/or image sets.

The **theme** element of a forum style is a grouping of formatting rules used to define the visual decoration of a forum. The most common uses of the theme are specifying the font face, colors, background colors, and borders of page elements. Theme elements can be difficult to locate because they can be stored in three different locations. Most styles store theme data in one or more **Cascading Style Sheet (CSS)** files, such as subsilver.css and formIE.css. The name of the CSS files will vary with each forum style, but many times, there will be at least one CSS file named after the forum style. Some styles will place their CSS formatting rules in the `overall_header.tpl` template file instead of a separate CSS file. Others may use a combination of the `overall_header.tpl` technique and database storage of some values. The subSilver style uses the combination method, but also includes a CSS file that can be used after a manual change.

An **image set** element includes all the images that are part of a style. Some examples are the folder images, voting result bar graphics, and language-specific buttons such as "Reply" and "New Topic." There are also images that may be used mainly for decorative purposes, such as background or header images. Decorative images are sometimes considered part of the theme, instead of the image set.

In addition to the template files already discussed, the template element can also contain two special configuration files related to the theme and image set elements. The theme configuration file, `theme_info.cfg`, is used for saving theme database data associated with a template. The saved data can then be imported into another forum's database later. For the most part, you will only rarely need to edit this file. It is usually automatically generated or provided as needed. The second configuration file holds template configuration data. In most cases, that will merely be a list of graphic files in the image set of a style. These template configuration files have a name based on their matching template, such as `subsilver.cfg`.

Style Storage

Details of all of the styles available on a forum are stored in the forum's SQL database. The database only holds a list of installed styles, the name of an associated template element for each style, and some limited theme data. No image set data is stored in your database.

On the other hand, style elements are stored in the `templates` directory of the forum file system. The `templates` directory contains subdirectories that are named uniquely and after each individual set of template files. Each subdirectory of `templates` will contain template, theme, image set, and configuration files for one or more styles. Until new styles are installed or created, the only subdirectory in `templates` will be `subsilver`.

In most cases, a `templates` directory will contain two other subdirectories: `admin` and `images`. The `admin` subdirectory will contain template files used to display the Administration Control Panel. The `images` subdirectory will hold the image set used in the style, and may have language-named subdirectories, such as `lang_english` or `lang_dutch`, for images that display typed text in different languages. Some more advanced styles may include directories other than `admin` and `images`.

Editing phpBB Files

Throughout this chapter, you will be learning about and using a new skill that will be very useful to you as the administrator of a phpBB forum. You have already learned about some of the powerful configurations and features available through the Administration Control Panel, but there are many more that are not found there. These features can only be accessed (or in some cases, added) by editing phpBB's files yourself. You must be careful to follow proper procedures when altering the files because phpBB is a delicate and complicated set of scripts. Doing so can save you a lot of headaches later, as many have learned first hand.

> You will be reminded of these procedures at several later points in the book. Try to follow them before manually editing any files, even if you are not reminded. This cannot be stressed enough, because these procedures can save you a lot of time when dealing with problems.

Before editing any file, the most important thing you should do is create a backup of that file. This simply means creating a copy of the file in its current condition. If you encounter problems due to your editing later, you can replace the edited file with the backup. That will effectively revert your forum to the pre-edited state of the file. At some point in your phpBB experience, you will definitely need to use a backup of a file. Everyone makes mistakes at some point, and it is nothing to be ashamed about. At other times, things simply do not work. Regardless of the cause, very few mistakes can be permanently fatal to a phpBB forum if you make backups before doing anything.

When you do edit a phpBB file, it is important to use the correct type of program. phpBB uses three types of files: graphics, text files containing program code, and text files containing display code. **Graphics** are standard image files you would see on any website and should be edited in programs such as Jasc Paint Shop Pro, Adobe Photoshop, or any other program capable of handling them. The text files, however, are special. Making a mistake in a graphic file will not damage your forum, but making one in a display code file or program code can easily cripple your forum.

All of phpBB's **program code files** contain the essential scripting needed to operate and display all aspects of a phpBB-powered forum and website. They are the backbone of phpBB. These files may have filename extensions of .php, .inc, or .cfg, and are plain text files created in a Unix text file format. This mainly means that when editing the files, you need to use a program capable of understanding the Unix text format. The majority of simple text-editing software will have no problems with this. Microsoft Notepad, perhaps the most commonly used text editor of the Microsoft Windows operating system, cannot understand the Unix format fully. It displays all the contents of a Unix text file on one long line, so Notepad is not the best choice for phpBB administrators. WordPad editor, also included with Microsoft Windows, can read Unix files without any problems. Most dedicated phpBB coders use more advanced text-editing programs with special features related to the PHP programming language. Some popular examples are EditPlus, TextPad, and PHPEdit, but there are many more available. You should, however, not need anything more complex than WordPad for the examples here.

The **display code files** are the .tpl files of the template element and the .css files of the theme element we learned about earlier. Like the program code files, these are plain text files saved in a Unix text file format. WordPad will again be our choice for editing these files for the examples in this chapter. There are special HTML-editing programs, such as Dreamweaver MX, which can be used to edit template files. Those programs tend to cause as many problems as they solve, so you may want to avoid them for now unless you are very familiar with the program you choose.

Finally, there is one more note about editing both program and display code files. When saving these files, you need to make certain to save them in the proper file format. These are supposed to be plain text files, so you must save them as that. To save an edited phpBB file in WordPad, just click the Save toolbar icon or select Save from the File menu. WordPad should automatically save the file correctly. If you must select Save As, make certain to choose Text Document in the Saves as type selection list.

> Microsoft WordPad may be able to read Unix file formats, but it does not save files in that format. Instead, it saves files in a **personal computer (PC)** format.

Installing a New Style

One of the easiest ways to customize the appearance of your forum is to download and install a new phpBB style. Hundreds of different styles have been created based on topics like color schemes, popular movies, television shows, hobbies, sports, etc. The majority of these styles are free to download and use, although there are also some commercial styles and style designers available. Some websites that offer style downloads also provide demonstration forums in which you can preview any of the styles without downloading anything. Two of the best websites for downloading phpBB styles are:

- The phpBB Styles Database:
  http://www.phpbb.com/styles/.
- The phpBBHacks Templates Database:
  http://www.phpbbhacks.com/templates.php.

Remember, some online communities use the terms template or theme when referring to a complete style, rather than names of style elements. phpBBHacks.com tends to use template in this manner.

Be certain to select a style that is compatible with the version of phpBB that you are using. The two sites above will list the compatible phpBB versions for each style, but other sites may not. Also keep in mind that some other sites carry styles for special ported versions of phpBB that are used with content management systems like PHP-Nuke. Those styles will *not* be compatible with an original flavor phpBB forum and vice versa.

Once you have selected and downloaded a new style, you will need to install the style to your forum. The installation is not a hard process if everything is prepared properly. You will, however, find it a bit daunting if the process or the creation of the style has been handled incorrectly.

Most downloads will come in a ZIP file format. Before you can install a downloaded style, you need to decompress the ZIP file. If you downloaded phpBB in a ZIP file, you are most probably already familiar with decompressing a file. Even if you are not, there are many decompression software programs you can download. Some of the more famous names include WinZip, WinAce, and WinRAR. Some, like ZipGenius (http://www.zipgenius.it/) or XAce, are free. WinZip has a Wizard mode that is very easy to use, so we will not look at decompression in great detail here.

Creating a Copy Style

For the purposes of illustration, this chapter will discuss the usage of a sample style called subBook. Instead of downloading and uncompressing this style, it was created as a quickly renamed copy of the subSilver style. If you would like to create your own subBook style so you can follow along, follow these simple instructions.

Time For Action—Creating a Copy Style

1. Make a copy of the templates/subSilver directory. The copy should contain all the same files found under subsilver.
2. Change the name of the copy directory to subBook.
3. Rename the subsilver.cfg and subsilver.css files to subBook.cfg and subBook.css, respectively.
4. Open the theme_info.cfg file for editing. In this file, you will see subsilver used several times. Change each of these instances to subBook. Take care that you do not delete or change anything else in the file. Remember to follow the proper editing procedures you learned earlier.

5. The name of the subSilver style is referenced in around forty to fifty lines inside template files in your subBook directory. The exact files and number of times vary depending on the version of phpBB 2.0 you are using. When creating a new style from subSilver as we are doing, you need to change all these references to the name of the new style (subBook in our case). Clearly, this step will take some time. This will not affect our installation or uninstallation examples, so you may skip most of this for now. Some advanced text editors have special search and replace features that can help you do this more quickly. At the very least, do these steps on the overall_header.tpl file.

6. Save and close all open files.

What Just Happened?

Every style available for phpBB is based around a set of files stored in the templates directory. The easiest way to create a new style is to copy the files of another and make a few changes to some of the copied files. These files are the configuration files, such as subsilver.cfg and theme_info.cfg, which phpBB uses for installing and managing styles. The Cascading Style Sheet file, subsilver.css in this case, was also renamed. As a result, references to subsilver.css in overall_header.tpl also had to be changed to the new name of that file. Completing these steps gives you a new style, which you can edit as much as you like without affecting your forums' other styles.

Installing One Element at a Time

Once you have a new style to install, either from downloading or copying subsilver, you need to place that style's directories and files into the templates directory of your forum. phpBB's Administration Control Panel can automatically detect all styles placed into this directory. If your forum is on a remote server, as most forums and websites tend to be, then you will have to upload the directories and files to that server via one of the methods supported by your web hosting company. This is usually through **File Transfer Protocol (FTP)**, SSH, or some other setup. Once you have copied or placed the files into templates, you have completed two thirds of the style installation already:

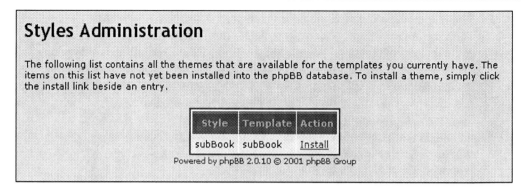

With the new style's files placed in your forum file system, you are now ready to install the style through phpBB's Administration Control Panel. Log in to your forum using an administrator account and enter the Control Panel. In the navigation menu frame, scroll down to the Styles Admin section. There are several options here; we are only interested in the Add link for the moment. Click this link to enter the Styles Administration page.

The Styles Administration page lists all the uninstalled styles phpBB has detected in your templates directory. You may notice that this page uses both **theme** and **style** to refer to the styles. This confusion stems from the fact that we have already installed the image set and template style elements simply by placing them into the templates directory. All that remains is to install the theme element, and thereby complete the style's installation. To install a theme, just click the Install link next to the entry in the list. phpBB will now show the style in the drop-down selection list found in user profiles and the phpBB configuration page:

Posts for Popular Threshold	25
Default Style	subSilver
Override user style Replaces users style with the default	subBook subSilver No
Default Language	English

Troubleshooting

phpBB is a complicated set of scripts, so even something that should be simple, like installing a style, can cause you problems. There are many causes of these problems, ranging from designer mistakes to errors in the copying of the files, but all of them are easy to fix. Let us examine some of the more common troubles encountered by forum administrators in the past.

Style Does Not Appear in Administration

If a style does not appear in the Styles Administration page after you have copied it to the templates directory, there is usually a problem with the theme_info.cfg file that should be in the style's directory. Make sure this file has been copied and that the name of the file has not been changed. If the file is present and named correctly, then there is a problem inside the file itself. Some styles have been distributed with errors in this file.

Open theme_info.cfg for editing. It should resemble the subSilver file shown in the figure that follows. Note that each line begins with $subsilver[0], followed by other characters. The subsilver part is extremely important, and must be spelled in exactly the same manner as the name of the style's templates directory and cannot contain any spaces. The name will be different for each template, of course. phpBB will consider all of these to be completely different things:

- subSilver
- sub silver
- Subsilver
- SubSilver
- subsilver

This screenshot shows a portion of an unaltered subSilver theme_info.cfg. Only our first option, subSilver, would be correct in this instance. Check each line of theme_info.cfg and make any corrections needed to the file or, if necessary, rename the style's templates directory. In certain cases, the latter will be an easier method of correcting the problem. Other styles will have different names for their directory and in theme_info.cfg, but the name must be the same in both places.

Configuration File Cannot Be Opened

Sometimes phpBB may have trouble finding the configuration file for a template element. When this happens, either during installation or normal forum operations, the forum will present the user with a Critical Error message, as shown in the following figure, mentioning the name of the template. That name is a very important part of this error message, because it is telling you what name phpBB has used to look for the configuration file. When the name of the template is shown as subSilver, phpBB could not find a file called subSilver.cfg in the templates/subSilver directory. Similarly, the name subBook means phpBB looked for subBook.cfg in the templates/subBook directory. The pattern here should be clear:

> phpBB : Critical Error
>
> Could not open subSilver template config file

To repair this error, you need to ensure that phpBB can find the file in question. As with the error when the style does not appear in Styles Administration, the names of the actual file and directory must be exactly the same as that in the error message. Subbook is not the same as subBook. First, look in the templates directory and ensure that there is a subdirectory with the template name. Next, look inside that subdirectory for the template configuration file. If either the directory or file is named incorrectly, renaming them to the correct spelling should fix the error.

If there is no templates subdirectory that comes even close to having the correct name, there are two ways to fix the error temporarily. The first method is to rename another subdirectory (and the template configuration file inside it) to the name phpBB is trying to find. When doing this, be sure to write down the original name for a quick change-back later. The second and better method is to copy another template and rename it. The steps for this are the same as those in the *Creating a Copy Style* section earlier in this chapter, except you will not need to edit theme_info.cfg. With the problem repaired for the moment, you can try to uninstall the problem style or work out a more lasting solution like replacing the templates files of the style.

Removing an Installed Style

At some point, you may decide that you want to remove a style you have added to your phpBB forum. This is a much simpler process than installing styles. There are two steps to removing a style: deleting the style and theme information from the database and deleting the `templates` directory of the style.

In the Administration Control Panel, scroll the navigation menu down to the Styles Admin section. Clicking the Management link will load a Styles Administration page, listing the styles currently installed on your forum. It looks very similar to the installation page you have already seen. By clicking the Delete link next to a style, you will remove all information related to that style in your forum's SQL database. You will be asked to confirm the deletion before it actually happens. Any users that have selected a style in their profiles will automatically have their selection changed when that style is deleted. Their profile setting will be altered to the style selected as the Board Default on the General Configuration page of the Administration Control Panel.

> If you only have one style installed on your forum, you cannot delete it. You also cannot delete the Board Default style.

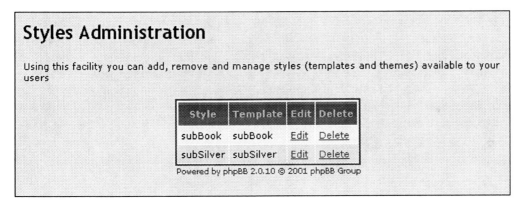

The second aspect of removing a style calls for deleting that style's related subdirectory of the `templates` directory. This will typically be done through the same means by which you copied the style into `templates` when installing it. Since it is possible to have multiple styles that use a single template or image set element with different themes, you should make certain that removing these files will not damage any styles you have not deleted in the Administration Control Panel.

Create or Customize

So far, we have only looked at installing new styles that already exist. This is only one of the ways in which we can alter the appearance of a phpBB, however. Two of our other options are creating a completely new style or customizing one already installed, like subSilver. Both of these options have some benefits and some drawbacks.

Creating a new style can really bring life to a forum. If your forum has a look that is unlike any other, your visitors are more likely to remember it. You probably remember some of the unique-looking websites you have visited in the past yourself. Also, you do not have to spend time looking through hundreds of existing styles for something you like or one that will fit nicely with the subject matter of your forum. Sometimes you may not even be able to find a style appropriate to your subject! The temptation to create your own style is great.

On the other hand, creating a new style is a lot of work! There are many graphics required for normal phpBB operations, and you will probably want to replace most of them with your own. You may even want to create new graphics and alter the template files to create new visual effects. Essentially, you would be designing an entire website. If you are not an experienced web designer or graphic artist, you may find the task to be a bit beyond your current skill level.

When you customize an existing style, you will save a lot of time over creating a new one. The existing structure will already be complete, other than any changes you want to make. You can quickly replace any images or colors to alter the mood of the forum, as you will see later in this chapter. The work of the original style creator will serve as a guideline to help you develop your knowledge. Then again, if you customize a style, that same existing structure will limit you unless changed greatly. Chances are that the customized style will bear some resemblance to the original, and many people will know that at first glance.

So which method is better? It really depends on how much you want to change the look of a forum. There is a good chance you can find an existing style to customize that will not limit you too much. If you look at enough styles, however, you will find that many of them are based, at least in part, on the original subSilver style. For something unique, you will have to create a new style.

In the rest of this chapter, we will learn to customize an existing style. However, the examples will use the subBook style created earlier in the chapter. This approach will allow us to preserve the original subSilver style of your forum, while making any changes we choose to the subBook copy.

If you did not create and install subBook earlier or replace all the uses of the subSilver name in subBook's template files, you may wish to do so now. You can work with subSilver if you like.

Customizing through the Stylesheet

The quickest way to overhaul the look of a forum is to change its colors, fonts, and other visual (but non-graphical) decorations. When we looked at the basic elements of a style earlier, we learned that a theme defines and controls these concepts through the formatting rules of a **Cascading Style Sheet (CSS)**. CSS formatting rules add stylistic data, such as specifications for fonts, colors, sizes, borders, and spacing to a document structured with a markup language like HTML. Since phpBB creates documents of this kind to display a forum, the preferred method for changing these parts of the outward appearance of the forum is CSS.

CSS rules can be stored in three different places: in an external CSS file such as subBook.css, in overall_header.tpl, or in a combination of the overall_header.tpl method with some database storage. subSilver uses the combination method, and therefore subBook will also do the same.

Editing the Stylesheet in the Admin Panel

We can look at the database storage portion of the combination method first. It allows us to edit certain aspects of the stylesheet through the Administration Control Panel. The values entered into the administration feature are placed into the SQL database and later retrieved for use on every page phpBB displays.

To access the stylesheet-editing tool, visit the Styles Admin section of the Administration Control Panel, and click the Management link. This loads the same Styles Administration page you saw when exploring the means of removing installed styles. However, we are now interested in the Edit link instead of the Delete link. Clicking Edit will load the Edit Theme page, which provides a simple form for changing colors, fonts, text sizes, and a few other theme aspects.

Time For Action—Editing the Stylesheet
1. Locate the line labeled Background Color on the page.
2. There is a form field on this line containing the text E5E5E5. Delete that text.
3. Type CC0000 in the form field. Use the number zero, not the capital letter O.

4. Scroll down to the bottom of the page and press the Save Settings button.

5. On the next page, click the word Here in the text Click Here to return to Style Administration. This returns you to the Styles Administration page, where your change will be reflected.

What Just Happened?

As the name suggests, the Edit Theme page allows you to alter some aspects of the forum's theme. Each aspect that can be altered has a matching form field, such as Background Color for the background color of forum pages. By replacing E5E5E5 with CC0000, you altered the page background color from a light gray to red. If you replace CC0000 with E5E5E5 and Save Settings again, the change will be reversed.

Editing Other Theme Components

You can change more than just the background color of pages. The first two options on the Edit Theme page actually allow you to modify two aspects of the style, even though Theme may be used in their labels. Alterations to the Theme Name will be reflected in board style selection lists and Styles Administration. Selecting a new Template can change the entire layout of a forum while keeping the current color scheme. All templates in your forum's templates directory will be listed in this selection box, even if they are not currently used in an installed style.

The remaining thirty eight options are presented in a three-column format. The first column, Theme Element, describes the individual settings while the second column holds the current values. When you install a new style, some values may or may not be provided automatically; it varies from style to style. These two columns are the most relevant to your needs.

The third column, Simple Name, can hold some extra descriptive information about the use of these settings. If you look at the Edit Theme page for subSilver, you can see this in action. Unfortunately, phpBB does not have a method of importing Simple Name data when installing new styles, so this column is often ignored. You can enter short descriptions of your own, but otherwise only subSilver will use this column:

Edit Theme

In the form below you can edit the settings for the selected theme

Theme Settings		
Theme Name:	subBook	
Template:	subBook ▾	

Theme Element	Value	Simple Name
CSS Stylesheet: Filename for CSS stylesheet to use for this theme.	subBook.css	
Background Image:		
Background Colour:	E5E5E5	
Text Colour:	000000	
Link Colour:	006699	
Visited Link Colour:	5493B4	
Active Link Colour:		

Since there are so many options on this page, let us concentrate on the types of values that can be entered, the settings used most often, and the ones you would most likely want to change. Many settings are alternative versions of others, so looking at every single one in detail is not necessary. All of the options are listed in a table at the end of this section.

Not all templates will use every setting in the same way. Some templates also do not use all of the settings provided. You should consider the descriptions provided here as a general guide to the ways the settings *can* be used, but not how they *must* be used. There is a fair amount of flexibility here, and some templates make use of that.

Allowed Values

There are several types of values that can be entered and most settings accept only one type. Those restricted to one kind of value can be grouped under filename, color, font size, and font face settings. All other settings accept filename, color, and CSS class name values, but only one kind of value can be used in each group of these settings.

The filename settings—CSS Stylesheet and Background Image—should only be used with the names of existing files in the `templates` directory of a style. It is possible to use a file that is not in a `templates` subdirectory, but this often requires some editing of multiple template files. Some styles, including subSilver, will not use one or both of this pair when first installed. Make sure a value is filled in for CSS Stylesheet regardless, as you may find yourself needing it later. Background Image is optional.

Color settings require a hexadecimal color code. Hexadecimal color codes, sometimes called HTML color codes, are combinations of six letters and numbers that represent a color, usually prefaced with a pound symbol (#). Many websites provide charts and lists that show examples of these codes. When entering a hexadecimal color code into the color settings of this page, you must not include the pound symbol. The color settings will accept only six character values, so including the pound will cause the last character of the code to be cut off! That can lead to some weird color effects. You may be tempted to enter a color name, such as red or green, for the color settings. If you do so, however, you will get some strange results. Lists of the different hexadecimal codes are available on many websites. Two good lists can be found at `http://www.htmlgoodies.com/tutors/colors.html` and `http://webmonkey.wired.com/webmonkey/reference/color_codes/`.

Font size settings are limited to simple integer numbers like 9, 10, or 15. These will usually be related to a font size in pixel or point measurements, but the type of measurement can vary with each style. Since some styles may also use percentage measurements, you may want to leave these settings alone until you have determined the type of units used in the stylesheet.

The last of the restricted value settings—font faces—accepts comma-separated lists of typeface names. An example of a good value is Verdana, Arial, Helvetica, sans-serif. If you want to include a name that consists of more than one word in the list, place it inside single or double quotes: for example, 'Verdana', 'Trebuchet MS'. You can also use a single name, but it is a better idea to use a list. When a list is provided, the first font that is installed on the viewer's computer will be used.

The more flexible settings allow you to use filenames, colors, or CSS class names for values, as already stated. Filename values operate under the same restrictions as those for filename-specific settings. Color values can be hexadecimal color codes, including the pound symbol this time, or simple names like blue. **CSS class names** are names of Cascading Style Sheet formatting rules. They will usually be short names made of all lowercase letters and numbers. The formatting rules named will be used to control the display of everything that the theme element controls.

Commonly Used and Altered Elements

You have already learned about a few settings, such as font sizes and faces, in the previous section. Now let us examine some more useful options in the Edit Theme page.

Table Cell Colors

The Table Cell Color 1, Table Cell Color 2, Table Cell Class 1, and Table Cell Class 2 elements are interesting because they are perhaps the most commonly used. Any aspect of phpBB that displays data in table rows, such as the member list, forums, and topics, can use these elements to achieve an alternating row color effect. For compatibility with phpBB's internal coding, Table Cell Class 1 often has a value of row1 and Table Cell Class 2 a value of row2. This is a sort of unspoken standard, but one that is not always used.

Font Colors

Two options that many forum administrators like to change, but often cannot locate without help, are Font Color 2 and Font Color 3. All font color settings are used to color a variety of text, but these two are used for the special colors given to administrator and moderator usernames on the forum in several locations like online user lists. Font Color 3 assigns the administrator names' color, and Font Color 2 details moderator name color.

Again, these colors are used in other places as well, so be sure to look around the forum if you change them. It is very easy to change the name colors to something nice only to find your table headers or code BBCodes have become unreadable.

Once you have edited the elements to your preferences, you should click the Save Settings button at the bottom of the Edit Theme page to store the new values in the database. You will be shown a confirmation message that the settings have been updated, and the new settings should be reflected on any page loaded after that message.

The following table lists the names of theme elements and defines them:

Theme Element Name	Description
CSS Stylesheet	Filename for a Cascading Style Sheet file.
Background Image	Image used as a background for the forum. Not used in subSilver.
Background Color	Color of page backgrounds.
Text Color	Default text color of all pages.
Link Color	Default color of all unvisited links.

Theme Element Name	Description
Visited Link Color	Color for all links that have been visited.
Active Link Color	When clicking a link, it switches color. Not used in subSilver.
Hover Link Color	When moving the mouse pointer over a link it changes to this color.
Table Row Color 1	Background color for table rows, often very light.
Table Row Color 2	Another, usually medium, table row background color.
Table Row Color 3	Third row background color, rarely used and is often the darkest.
Table Row Class 1	CSS class name for table rows. Not used in subSilver.
Table Row Class 2	Class name for a second set of rows. Not used in subSilver.
Table Row Class 3	Class name for a third row set. Not used in subSilver.
Table Header Color 1	Color for table headings. Also used for page borders in subSilver.
Table Header Color 2	Second heading color. Also used for table borders in subSilver.
Table Header Color 3	Third heading color. Also used for inner table borders in subSilver.
Table Header Class 1	CSS class name for table heading cells.
Table Header Class 2	Class name for a second set of table heading cells.
Table Header Class 3	Class name for a third heading set.
Table Cell Color 1	Background color of various common table cells.
Table Cell Color 2	Alternative table cell background color.
Table Cell Color 3	Another table cell background color. Not used in subSilver.
Table Cell Class 1	CSS Class name for table cells. Often used to alternate row colors.
Table Cell Class 2	Second Class name for cells. Often used to alternate row colors.
Table Cell Class 3	Third possible class name. Not used in subSilver.

Theme Element Name	Description
Font Face 1	Default type face for most text.
Font Face 2	Second type face, sometimes for topic titles.
Font Face 3	Third type face. Often used for code BBCode tags.
Font Size 1	Smallest font size.
Font Size 2	Medium font size.
Font Size 3	Largest font size, used for most text, including posts.
Font Color 1	Quote BBCode text color.
Font Color 2	Code BBCode text color. Also moderator username color.
Font Color 3	Table header cell text color. Also administrator user name color.
Span Class 1	A CSS class name for use in HTML span tags. Not used in subSilver.
Span Class 2	Another class name for span tags. Not used in subSilver.
Span Class 3	Third class name for span tags. Not used in subSilver.

Changing CSS Styles to Change the Look of Your Site

The second portion of the combined stylesheet storage method deals with CSS-formatting rules placed in the overall_header.tpl file of a template. These formatting rules, or **CSS classes**, control many aspects of the forum's display. By editing the CSS classes directly, you can create a broader range of design changes than are possible through the Edit Theme utility.

The first step is to locate the CSS classes in templates/subBook/overall_header.tpl. Open that file in WordPad and scroll down to a line that contains <style type= "text/css">. All of the CSS classes are between this line and another containing </style>. Each of the classes has two major parts: a class name, also known as a selector, and a declaration block.

The **class name** is a short and descriptive name that will be used to associate the individual classes with elements of forum pages. Names may be the same as those of HTML tags, such as body, td, hr, or font, or author-created names preceded by a period, such as .postbody or .quote. A combination of the two, such as td.row1 is also acceptable. You will also see classes containing names separated by commas; this is a shortcut for applying one class to all of the named elements.

Declaration blocks consist of one or more declaration lines enclosed in curly brackets. Each **declaration line** holds a property name and value separated by a colon and ends with a semicolon. Several declaration lines can actually be placed on one line of text, as long as a semicolon ends each declaration, and you will see several such cases in the files. Property names and values specify the actual formatting features like colors, borders, and so on. Here is a sample line for underlining text:

```
text-decoration: underline;
```

Most styles' stylesheets will also include comment lines starting with /* and ending with */ that explain what display elements of the forum each class will affect. Comment lines do not affect any layout features themselves. An entire class might resemble this sample.

```
td.row2
{
    color: black;
    /* White Background */
    background-color: #FFFFFF;
}
```

Until you reach a point where you are adding new features to your forum, you should not need to alter class names very much, if at all. On the other hand, editing the declaration blocks will let you do just about anything. By examining the existing entries in the file, you will get a good idea of what you can do by adding or removing declaration lines in each class.

Hundreds of possible combinations of property names and values exist. There are also some types of class names not covered here or used in subSilver and subBook. For more information about Cascading Style Sheets beyond the scope of this book, check out these resources:

184 Manually selected Style Sheet Resources:
http://www.cbel.com/style_sheets/

W3Schools CSS Tutorials: http://www.w3schools.com/css/

css-discuss Wiki http://css-discuss.incutio.com/

In overall_header.tpl, you will see many declaration lines containing special **template variables** like {T_BODY_BGCOLOR}. Template variables are a special feature of phpBB used to substitute data into the layout generated from the template files. Some recognizable characteristics of template variables are names beginning and ending with curly brackets and containing only letters, numbers, underscores, and periods. You will not see template variables whose names contain semicolons, colons, or most other special characters. Any template variables in the stylesheet will be replaced with the "theme element" values of the Edit Theme utility; they are where the combination of the database and overall_header.tpl come into play. For a listing of the template variables and their matching theme element names, consult the table at the end of this section.

Template variables can be applied to classes for other types of theme elements, as well. For an example, look at the first class in subBook's overall_header.tpl. This body class, which affects the HTML <body> tag and thus an entire webpage, uses several table color elements in scrollbar-related declaration lines. These lines will change the colors in certain parts of your web browser's scrollbar, if the browser supports them. The scrollbar properties are not part of the standard CSS features and only function in certain browsers, such as Microsoft's Internet Explorer. Netscape and Mozilla browsers ignore the scrollbar properties.

For an interesting example of how you can change the look of your forum, locate the .bodyline class. This would be on a single line about eight lines below the body class. Near the end of the line, you can see the border property, which manages the border around the forum pages. It should currently have values that create a solid, one pixel wide, light blue border, with the color changeable in Edit Theme. Now, replace the word solid with dashed. Save this change and look at your forum's index page—it now has a dashed line for a border. You can also try dotted, ridge, and groove for some other effects. By altering the number portion of the 1px code in the same area, you can increase and decrease the width of the border. Try 10px and dotted together for an unusual view.

> The stylesheet code found in subBook/overall_header.tpl is duplicated in subBook/simple_header.tpl and, with some changes, in subBook/admin/page_header.tpl. Any changes applied to one file should also be made in the others, if you want to keep the same look across all parts of the forum.

Using External Stylesheets

By placing a stylesheet in overall_header.tpl, phpBB gives you a lot of control through the Edit Theme page, but it comes at a cost. The stylesheet has to be freshly loaded on every page, and this can slow down a very busy forum. An alternative is to use an external stylesheet file, such as subSilver.css and subBook.css. Web browsers do not refresh external stylesheets as often, resulting in smaller page sizes and faster loading times. This type of stylesheet does not support the Edit Theme utility, however, so the utility is rendered almost useless. Edit Theme will still control administrator and moderator username colors and, depending on the style, row classes and colors.

To enable the external stylesheet for subBook, find the following line in templates/subBook/overall_header.tpl:

```
<!-- link rel="stylesheet"
href="templates/subBook/{T_HEAD_STYLESHEET}" type="text/css" -->
```

This line is an HTML comment line due to the !-- and -- character sequences near the beginning and end. Like the Cascading Style Sheet comment lines, it has no effect on the page layout. By removing the comment characters, you can have the line become a reference to the external stylesheet file. The line should then look like this:

```
<link rel="stylesheet" href="templates/subBook/{T_HEAD_STYLESHEET}"
type="text/css">
```

You should also delete all the CSS classes in overall_header.tpl, or they will override the same classes in the external stylesheet. If you have made any changes to those CSS classes, make identical changes in subBook.css before deleting the code from overall_header.tpl. You will find the same classes in subBook.css, but you cannot use template variables in external stylesheet files. If you make these same changes in simple_header.tpl and admin/page_header.tpl, you can control the appearance of the entire forum from a single stylesheet file. Note that the final line in admin/page_header.tpl will be slightly different. You need to add ../ before templates in this line for the stylesheet to be displayed properly on pages using this file. Those pages are generally Administration Control Panel pages, which only you may see (unless you give other users administrator access). The final line for admin/page_header.tpl is:

```
<link rel="stylesheet"
href="../templates/subBook/{T_HEAD_STYLESHEET}" type="text/css">
```

The following table lists the template variables and related theme elements:

Template Variable	Theme Element Name
{T_HEAD_STYLESHEET}	CSS Stylesheet
{T_BODY_BACKGROUND}	Background Image
{T_BODY_BGCOLOR}	Background Color
{T_BODY_TEXT}	Text Color
{T_BODY_LINK}	Link Color
{T_BODY_VLINK}	Visited Link Color
{T_BODY_ALINK}	Active Link Color

Template Variable	Theme Element Name
{T_BODY_HLINK}	Hover Link Color
{T_TR_COLOR1}	Table Row Color 1
{T_TR_COLOR2}	Table Row Color 2
{T_TR_COLOR3}	Table Row Color 3
{T_TR_CLASS1}	Table Row Class 1
{T_TR_CLASS2}	Table Row Class 2
{T_TR_CLASS3}	Table Row Class 3
{T_TH_COLOR1}	Table Header Color 1
{T_TH_COLOR2}	Table Header Color 2
{T_TH_COLOR3}	Table Header Color 3
{T_TH_CLASS1}	Table Header Class 1
{T_TH_CLASS2}	Table Header Class 2
{T_TH_CLASS3}	Table Header Class 3
{T_TD_COLOR1}	Table Cell Color 1
{T_TD_COLOR2}	Table Cell Color 2
{T_TD_COLOR3}	Table Cell Color 3
{T_TD_CLASS1}	Table Cell Class 1
{T_TD_CLASS2}	Table Cell Class 2
{T_TD_CLASS3}	Table Cell Class 3
{T_FONTFACE1}	Font Face 1
{T_FONTFACE2}	Font Face 2
{T_FONTFACE3}	Font Face 3
{T_FONTSIZE1}	Font Size 1
{T_FONTSIZE2}	Font Size 2
{T_FONTSIZE3}	Font Size 3

Template Variable	Theme Element Name
{T_FONTCOLOR1}	Font Color 1
{T_FONTCOLOR2}	Font Color 2
{T_FONTCOLOR3}	Font Color 3
{T_SPAN_CLASS1}	Span Class 1
{T_SPAN_CLASS2}	Span Class 2
{T_SPAN_CLASS3}	Span Class 3

Customizing through Images

Another major part of a forum's appearance is created using images. **Forum images** can be divided into two main categories: those that are just for looks, and those that serve some function. The former might include a forum's logo or menu link images, while examples of the latter would be new post indicators and posting buttons. By replacing any of these images, you can create a new user interface and adapt your forum's design at the same time. If you are a graphic artist or experienced in creating your own images, you can create some awesome images to liven up your forum.

You can also download new graphics from phpBB communities, of course. Both phpBB.com and phpBBHacks.com, which offer style downloads as mentioned previously, also offer some graphic sets. Some of their image downloads are rank and emoticon images, but you can find packs of normal forum buttons too. A few style authors have also made special PSD image packs available, which can be used to create new images for their styles using Adobe Photoshop and other image editors. PSD packs for styles you install, if available, may be useful when adding new features to your forum later.

Installing New Images to Change the Look of Your Site

There are two ways to install new images to a phpBB forum. The first is to replace an existing image. Replacing an image entails finding or creating an image, renaming it with the same filename as an image already used on your forum, deleting the existing image, and putting the new image in the same location. This is a quick way of getting new graphics on your forum, but it will limit you to the same type of image previously in place. If you have a JPEG image, like a digital photo, that you want to use for a New Topic button in subSilver or subBook, you would have to convert it to a GIF image, losing some picture quality in the process. For cases like this, it's better to use the second method of installing new images: adding an image with a new filename. In order to get phpBB to detect the new filename, however, you may have to edit the template configuration file of the style in which you are installing the new image. If you will recall from earlier in the chapter, these files have a name matching that of a `templates` subdirectory, such as `subSilver.cfg` or `subBook.cfg`, and list many of the graphics found on a forum. The entries in this list usually resemble these examples:

```
$images['name'] = "$current_template_images/image.gif";
$images['name'] = "$current_template_images/{LANG}/image.gif";
```

If you open `subBook.cfg` in WordPad, you should see several lines in this format. Generally speaking, you should only edit the parts of a line after the last backslash and before the last quotation mark, which would be `image.gif` in the example. If your new image is not inside the `images` subdirectory of the style's directory, like `templates/subBook/images`, then you would need to replace `$current_template_images` with the correct path to the image. It is usually easier to simply put the new file in the style's `images` directory. The special `{LANG}` placeholder allows phpBB to use different versions of an image in support of multiple languages.

The one image you might expect to find in the configuration file—the forum's phpBB logo—is actually not there. To change the filename for the logo, you will have to edit `overall_header.tpl`. The HTML image tag for the logo resembles:

```
<img src="templates/subBook/images/logo_phpBB.gif" border="0"
alt="{L_INDEX}" vspace="1" />
```

Notice the phpBB logo is the `logo_phpBB.gif` file. Most people want to change the logo quickly, so this is a good file to experiment with replacing or renaming.

Hacking phpBB

Altering the look of your forum is only one aspect of customizations that you can perform with phpBB. For some interesting changes, you'll most likely want to add some completely new features to your forum. You may also want to remove some features that you do not plan to use. To add new features, remove existing features, or otherwise alter the abilities of a phpBB forum, you will have to edit the code of the PHP script files that are the heart of phpBB. You may also need to edit or add new template files to the styles installed on a forum, as well. The process of making these kinds of changes is called **modifying** or **hacking** phpBB.

MODs and Hacks

There are many sets of instructions for altering phpBB's features available at online phpBB communities. Such downloads may include step-by-step instructions for altering core phpBB files or the SQL database, adding new forum files, or any combination of those three categories. These downloads are commonly called MODs or Hacks. **Hack** was the original term used during the era of phpBB 1 and is still used extensively in some phpBB communities. With the advent of phpBB 2.0, the term **MODs**, from a shortened form of the word modifications, also became popular. To avoid confusion, the term **modification** will be used in this chapter.

phpBB Modification

What exactly does a modification include? That will depend on the scope of the modification. Very simple modifications typically include one text file containing instructions for altering an existing phpBB file. More complex modifications may also include new files to be added to phpBB and a special installer file. Some extremely complex modifications typically include all of these, plus already edited copies of the original phpBB files. All these files will be placed together in a compressed file, typically in the ZIP format.

While a group of developers created phpBB, modifications are typically the work of individual phpBB users that needed the effect created by the modification. phpBB is open source and released under the GNU General Public License so, it and any derivative works (like modifications) can be freely distributed to others at no charge. Modification authors make their works available to others in the hope that other forum administrators will benefit from them and eventually contribute back to the larger phpBB community. Therefore, there is a large and diverse group of modifications created in different coding methods and writing styles. Some modifications are also released in developmental stages, and you should be careful about using those. They often contain bugs, security holes, or incomplete features that may annoy your forum's visitors.

The best places to find large selections of phpBB modification downloads are:

- phpBBHacks.com: http://www.phpbbhacks.com/
- phpBB Official Site: http://www.phpbb.com/

Many modification authors will also release their works on their own websites or other phpBB communities. If possible, make sure you only download modifications described as compatible for the version of phpBB you are using. There are many releases of phpBB 1 and phpBB 2, but not all modifications will work with every phpBB release. phpBB 1 modifications, mainly found only at phpBBHacks.com now, will not work on any phpBB 2 release. Some phpBB 2 modifications will work only with early or later versions of phpBB 2.0.

Installing a Modification

When you find and download a modification you wish to install, you need to follow a series of steps to place the new code in your forum and activate it fully. Like many other things, the exact steps needed vary with each modification. There is a standard way of proceeding that is common to all modifications, however. To begin with, let's install this simple modification. It adds a button to each user's posts that allows others to quickly search for all posts by that user.

```
#
#-----[ OPEN ]------------------------------------------
#
templates/subSilver/viewtopic_body.tpl

#
#-----[ FIND ]------------------------------------------
#
            //--></script><noscript>{postrow.ICQ_IMG}</noscript></td>

#
#-----[ IN-LINE FIND ]----------------------------------
#
</noscript>

#
#-----[ IN-LINE AFTER, ADD ]-----------------------------
-
#
{postrow.SEARCH_IMG}

#
#-----[ SAVE/CLOSE ALL FILES ]---------------------------
---
#
# End
```

Time For Action—Installing a Small Modification

1. Locate the templates/subSilver/viewtopic_body.tpl file of your forum. Open this file in your text-editing program.

2. Use the text-editing program's search feature to locate this line of text in the file. In many programs, this feature can be accessed from the menus or by pressing *Ctrl+F* on Windows systems.
   ```
   //--></script><noscript>{postrow.ICQ_IMG}</noscript></td>
   ```

3. Now, locate the text </noscript> within that line.

4. Directly after </noscript>, type a space and the text {postrow.SEARCH_IMG}. The final version of the line should look like this example:
   ```
   //--></script><noscript>{postrow.ICQ_IMG}</noscript>
   {postrow.SEARCH_IMG}</td>
   ```

5. Save and close the file. If necessary, upload it to your website, replacing the existing file there. You may repeat all of these steps with the `templates/subBook/viewtopic_body.tpl` file, if you wish.

6. Go to your forum and look at any post. You should see a new Search image below the post.

What Just Happened?

Congratulations, you have just installed your first phpBB modification! The majority of modifications contain a series of instructions similar to those on the previous page. Authors intend you to use these instructions as a basic guide to adding the modification to your phpBB files. By placing a little bit of new code inside your `viewtopic_body.tpl` file, you have enabled the search button that can be shown with forum posts.

Installing a Downloaded Modification

After you have downloaded a modification that you wish to install, you must first decompress the downloaded file if it is a ZIP file or another archive file format. When you do so, one or more new files, and possibly directories containing more files, will be created. When there is only one file, it will typically be a simple text file that you can open in WordPad. The name of the file is usually `readme.txt`, `install.txt`, `install.mod`, or something like that. For the sake of example, let's use `install.txt`.

> If a modification contains an `install.mod` file, you may not be able to open this file by double clicking on it like other files. The file extension `.mod` has been used by a popular music file format for years, so music players like WinAMP usually try to open double clicked `.mod` files. In these cases, you will have to open the file through WordPad's File | Open menu.

The `install.txt` will contain all the instructions for installing the modification's changes, as well as the author's credits and notes about the changes. Larger modifications may include both a `readme.txt` and an `install.txt` file. In those cases, it's usually a good idea to examine `readme.txt` before doing anything else, as it may contain special instructions beyond those found in `install.txt`.

A few modifications are simply written out in paragraph form, but the majority use a common template of a header and simple commands called actions. The modification header will contain basic information such as the modification's name, version number, author, description, and an estimation of installation difficulty and time. Important notes about the modification and its history might also be found here, so be certain to read the header fully. **Actions** describe steps of the modification installation using a header containing a brief, descriptive name followed by one or more lines of code. Here is an example of an action header, as it may appear in a file of instructions.

```
#
#-----[ ACTION NAME ]----------------------------------------
#
```

The actual name of each action will replace the text ACTION NAME. There are many kinds of actions, each of which has a different meaning. When used in a set of instructions, action names are usually typed entirely in capital letters.

> Remember to back up any file you are instructed to alter before doing anything to that file. Refer to the *Editing phpBB Files* section earlier in this chapter if you need to refresh your memory.

The Copy Action

This action, labeled **Copy**, is an instruction to place files into certain new locations. Typically, the files to be copied are part of the modification and must be uploaded to your forum. Sometimes they already exist in the forum and just need to be moved, but special cases like that should be noted in the modification's instructions.

```
#
#-----[ COPY ]----------------------------------------
#
db_update.php to db_update.php
functions_new.php to includes/functions_new.php
templates/*.* to templates/subSilver/*.*
```

Above is an example of a typical Copy action. Each line lists a file to copy on the left and the destination of the copy on the right. Unless otherwise noted, the destination path will be relative to your forum's main directory. With the example, you would place db_update.php in the main directory, alongside viewtopic.php and profile.php, functions_new.php inside the includes/ directory, and all the files in the modification's templates/ directory inside the forum's templates/subSilver/ directory. The special notation *.* is a quick way of saying *all files within this directory*.

The SQL Action and Editing the Database

When a hack adds new features, they are often tracked in some manner by the SQL database of the forum. In order to get this working, you will need to make changes to the database. Modification authors will include these changes using one or more of three methods. The first method, and most popular in more recently created modifications, is to include an installer script file. Installer files are special files with a .php filename extension that can make database changes for you. They are typically named install.php or db_update.php, but the name can have some variety. To use these files, you normally only need to place them in your forum's directory structure (the Copy action handles that) and run the file.

This part might be confusing to you. People learning how to install modifications often ask, "What does it mean to *run* the file?" To run a .php file, you need to visit it in your web browser like a normal web page. A good comparison comes from thinking of your forum's viewtopic.php, which displays all topics. Every time you read a topic in the forum, you are running the viewtopic.php file. Just visiting your uploaded db_update.php file will begin the process of editing the database. Some complicated installers may walk you through several steps.

> Many installer scripts will not work unless you log in to the forum using an administrator account before running the file. Always be sure to log in first, and delete the installer file *immediately* after running. Leaving an installer script in place can be a major security risk!

A second method of including database changes is to place a list of SQL query commands in the installation instructions under an SQL action. The third method places the same kind of list in a separate text file, which might be named sql.txt or schema.sql. Other names are possible, but the important thing to note is that any file with an extension of .sql is a text file containing SQL queries. When either of these two methods is used, you will need to do one of two things: create your own installer script or run the changes manually.

It is not very hard to create your own installer script. In fact, there are generators that can create a db_update.php file for you! One such generator can be found at http://www.phpbbhacks.com/forums/db_generator.php. Simply copy the SQL queries from the SQL action or file and paste them into this or another generator, submit the form, and you will be presented with the code of a db_update.php file. You can download the file directly from that page, place it in your forum, and run the file in the same way you would run an author-supplied installer.

> Some SQL queries may not be compatible with db_update.php generators. These will usually produce installer scripts that display parse errors when run. If this happens, visit a friendly phpBB support forum and ask for help with making the queries compatible.

In order to make database changes manually, you can use phpMyAdmin or another similar database management utility. However, you may need to edit the SQL queries before you can do this. When you installed phpBB, you had an option to enter a database table prefix. phpBB uses the value of this option for the beginning of all database table names. Each query in a modification should mention a database table name such as phpbb_posts or phpbb_config. If your chosen table prefix were myforum_, you would need to change the table names to myforum_posts and myforum_config before using the queries. Installer script files will typically make this change automatically, so you should consider generating one if you are uncomfortable with this process. These are some queries as they might appear before and after changing the table prefix:

```
CREATE TABLE phpbb_tracker (
    tracker_id mediumint(8) DEFAULT '0' NOT NULL,
    tracker1 tinyint(1) DEFAULT '0' NOT NULL,
    tracker2 varchar(40) NOT NULL,
    PRIMARY KEY (tracker_id),
);
CREATE TABLE myforum_tracker (
    tracker_id mediumint(8) DEFAULT '0' NOT NULL,
    tracker1 tinyint(1) DEFAULT '0' NOT NULL,
    tracker2 varchar(40) NOT NULL,
    PRIMARY KEY (tracker_id),
);
INSERT INTO phpbb_tracker (tracker_id, tracker1, tracker2)
    VALUES (1, 3,'Some text');
INSERT INTO myforum_tracker (tracker_id, tracker1, tracker2)
    VALUES (1, 3,'Some text');
```

With the queries in the proper format, open phpMyAdmin and, if necessary, select your database in the left column. Click on the SQL tab or Query Window link. Either of these will load a page containing a large text box. Copy the SQL queries from the modification instructions or text file and paste them into this box. A click of the Go button should run the queries on the database automatically.

The Open Action

This simple action tells you the name and location of a file you need to edit. You should open this file in WordPad, or your favorite text-editing program, and be prepared to make changes to it. If you have not already backed up the file, do so now. All the other actions that follow an Open action should be preformed on the file listed in this action until you reach the end of the instructions or another Open action.

```
#
#-----[ OPEN ]-----------------------------------------
#
includes/functions.php
```

The Find Action

Each Find action is followed by one or more lines of code that should be contained within the file in the last Open action. Your goal is to locate this code, which is supposed to be an easy task. Most text-editing programs, including WordPad, have a Find or Search function that makes searching the entire file quick and easy. The Find function should be accessible through the menus of the program or, in Windows programs, by pressing *Ctrl+F*.

Unfortunately, there are some problems that can make finding lines a chore. First, several versions of phpBB have been released. Each version has certain code changes, so phpBB 2.0 will have some modifications for early releases where the Find code is very different than the code in the latest version. In these cases, it is often best if you do not install the modification unless the relevant changes between versions seem minor. Another problem is that some modifications try to find code that has been changed, or even removed, by other modifications already. Some authors have tried to bypass this problem by only listing the first few characters of each line to find. That practice has created yet another problem due to misinterpretation of the actions that follow Find instructions. Finally, some lines of code appear more than once in some files. You may need to edit only a specific appearance or all instances.

How can we solve these problems? Sometimes it is not very easy. If you cannot locate some Find code, the first solution to try is searching for smaller portions of the code. Suppose you have a hard time locating the line of this instruction:

```
#
#-----[ FIND ]---------------------------------------------
#
'SOME_TPL_VARIABLE' => $some_php_variable,
```

Looking for a key part of the line, like SOME_TPL_VARIABLE, may allow you to find the line even if it has already been changed by another modification or version of phpBB. The ability to adapt lines of code is a key skill when installing modifications and you may need to develop this skill over time.

When dealing with lines or blocks of code that appear in a file several times, keep in mind that most modifications are written based on a top-to-bottom order. Say you have instructions containing two Find commands for one file, with the code of the second appearing twice in the file. The author usually means for you to locate the first appearance following the code of the first Find command.

The Addition Actions

Three actions can add a new code to a file: **Before, Add**; **After, Add**; and **Replace With**. Each of these addition actions will always follow a Find action, and operate in reference to the code in the Find action. In the case of Before, Add actions, the code following the action should be placed into the file on a line before the code of the Find action. For After, Add actions, the codes go onto a line after the Find action's code. A Replace With action will delete the Find action's code and substitute the new code for the old.

For the most part, these are simple steps. There is one point about both Before, Add and After, Add actions that cannot be stressed enough, and that is *always place the new code on a new line, separate from all other code*. Some modification authors, as has been mentioned, include only partial lines of code in their Find actions. The problem with this practice is that modification users tend to add new code right after that in a Find action, on the same line.

This places new code right in the middle of the original code, creating a series of syntax errors that can make a forum inaccessible. If you always add code before or after Find code by inserting it on a completely new line, you should be able to avoid this problem.

To illustrate how the code of a file should look, here are some sample action sequences and the correct resulting code. For the sake of these examples, assume a file containing the following code has already been referenced in an Open action.

```php
<?php

$number1 = $number2 = $number3 = 0;
$number1 = $x + $y;
$number2 = $y + $z;

$total = $number1 + $number2 + $number3;
echo 'The total is: ' . $total;

?>
```

First, a simple Find and After, Add combination:

```
#
#-----[ FIND ]----------------------------------------
#
$number1 = $x + $y;
$number2 = $y + $z;
#
#-----[ AFTER, ADD ]----------------------------------
#
$number3 = $a + $b;
```

This sequence should create:

```
$number1 = $number2 = $number3 = 0;
$number1 = $x + $y;
$number2 = $y + $z;
$number3 = $a + $b;

$total = $number1 + $number2 + $number3;
```

A Find and Before, Add combination is next:

```
#
#-----[ FIND ]----------------------------------------
#
$number1 = $x + $y;
$number2 = $y + $z;
#
#-----[ BEFORE, ADD ]---------------------------------
#
$my_array = array('a' => 1, 'b'=> 2, 'x' => 3, 'y' => 4, 'z' => 5);
while( list($key, $value) = each($my_array) )
{
    $$key = $value;
}
```

After applying this sequence, the file would contain:

```
$number1 = $number2 = $number3 = 0;
$my_array = array('a' => 1, 'b'=> 2, 'x' => 3, 'y' => 4, 'z' => 5);
while( list($key, $value) = each($my_array) )
{
    $$key = $value;
}
$number1 = $x + $y;
$number2 = $y + $z;
```

A Find action followed by a Replace With action could be:

```
#
#-----[ FIND ]----------------------------------------
#
$total = $number1 + $number2 + $number3;
#
#-----[ REPLACE WITH ]--------------------------------
#
$average = ($number1 + $number2 + $number3) / 3;
```

That sequence would transform the end of the file into this snippet of code.

```
$average = ($number1 + $number2 + $number3) / 3;
echo 'The total is: ' . $total;

?>
```

Finally, here is another version of the earlier Find and After, Add sequence. This time, the Find action contains only portions of the lines. The result of applying the sequence should be the same as if the full lines were given.

```
#
#-----[ FIND ]----------------------------------------
#
$number1 =
$number2 =
#
#-----[ AFTER, ADD ]----------------------------------
#
$number3 = $a + $b;
```

The In-Line Actions

Despite what you have just learned about the importance of adding code on new lines, sometimes you will need to change a piece of code within a line. The In-Line actions are used for this. There are four of these: **In-Line Find**; **In-Line Before, Add**; **In-Line After, Add**; and **In-Line Replace With**. Ideally, you will see a Find action with a long line of code, followed by an In-Line Find with a short snippet of that line, then one of the other three In-Line actions. Use them just as you would their normal counterparts, but this time do not add the new code on a separate line. You will actually insert the code inside the current line. In several modifications that use In-Line actions, you may have to change a line in several different places.

Using the same short file above, here is an example of an In-Line Replace With action sequence that edits two parts of one line.

```
#
#-----[ FIND ]----------------------------------------
#
echo 'The total is: ' . $total;
#
#-----[ IN-LINE FIND ]-------------------------------------
#
 total
#
#-----[ IN-LINE REPLACE WITH ]-----------------------------------
---
#
 average
#
#-----[ IN-LINE FIND ]-------------------------------------
#
$total
#
#-----[ IN-LINE REPLACE WITH ]-----------------------------------
---
#
$average
```

That sequence alters the end of the file to look like:

```
$average = ($number1 + $number2 + $number3) / 3;
echo 'The average is: ' . $average;

?>
```

The Last Action

Almost every modification's instructions end with a variation of this action:

```
#
#-----[ SAVE/CLOSE ALL FILES ]-----------------------------------
---
#
# End
```

This is the last step of the instructions. It serves as a reminder to save your changes, close any remaining open files, and transfer edited files to your forum if necessary. Once you have done those things, you should be finished with the modification installation. You should thoroughly test the installation with your administrator account, a normal user account, and, if necessary, a moderator account. Many modifications add features that work differently for accounts with different permissions. For testing purposes, it is best if you only install one modification at a time. If you were to install three or four modifications simultaneously and you encounter an error in your forum, you might have a hard time tracking down the cause.

The following table provides a quick reference of the modification Action:

Action Name	Definition
Copy	Copies one or more files from one location to another.
SQL	Runs one or more SQL queries on your forum's database. These should usually be completed before installing the remainder of the modification.
Open	Opens the file in preparation for editing. Every action following this until the last action, or another Open action, should be performed on this file. It is followed by a single filename.
Find	This locates the code in the file and is followed by code.
After, Add	Places the following code *on a new line after* the code in the preceding Find action. It always follows a Find action.
Before, Add	Places the following code *on a new line before* the code in the preceding Find action. It always follows a Find action.
Replace With	Deletes the code found in the preceding Find action and puts the following code in its place. It always follows a Find action.
In-Line Find	Usually follows a Find action. Locates the following code inside a longer line of code.
In-Line After, Add	Places the following code *after* the code in the preceding In-Line Find, *on the same line of code*. It always follows an In-Line Find action.
In-Line Before, Add	Places the following code *before* the code in the preceding In-Line Find, *on the same line of code*. It always follows an In-Line Find action.
In-Line Replace With	Deletes the code in the preceding In-Line Find and put this code in its place on the same line of code. It always follows an In-Line Find action.
Save/Close All Files	Signals the end of file changes and reminds you to save your changes. It is always the last action of a modification.
Add SQL	This is an older form of the SQL action, with the same meaning as that action.

The Trouble with Templates

One very important aspect of modification installation remains, just when you thought you had finished it. When you install modifications, you will see that almost all of those modifying or adding template files will only mention the subSilver template in their instructions. By this time, you should have installed at least one other template on your forum. With so many templates existing, it is not practical for authors to mention all of them in their instructions. Since every phpBB forum has subSilver installed at some point, and many templates are built from subSilver, only that one template gets mentioned, with an unspoken understanding that it is really a reference to all templates.

The trouble with templates is that you have to install every modification's template file changes to all your installed templates, even though the instructions do not tell you to do this. Also, if you install modifications and later install new templates, you have to apply the modifications to those templates. Should you forget to modify a template, any forum members using that template will not be able to access the modification's features unless they switch to another that you did edit.

Another problem in this area is the code of the templates themselves. While many templates are created from subSilver, quite a few are not. The latter kinds tend to have some very different markup language coding in their files. It can seem nearly impossible to locate code in a Find action unless you break it down into individual template variables. You might actually have to rewrite the new template files or code to match the look of the alternative templates, too. It can be quite a headache.

Uninstalling Modifications

Occasionally, you may have a need to remove a modification after installing it. Maybe you've found that two modifications are conflicting with each other or a modification does not live up to your expectations. Whatever the reason, uninstalling tends to be easier than installing.

There are two methods of removing a modification's changes to your files. Since you created backups before editing any of your files, you can replace your current files with those backup copies. This reverts the forum's files to the same condition they were in before the modification was installed. If you have made changes to the files other than installing this modification, then you should not restore the backup files. Doing so in such a case will cause your other changes to be lost.

The second method is to go through the modification's instructions as if installing, but invert the action commands. For example, if the instructions have a Find action followed by an After, Add action, you would locate and delete the After, Add code. In the case of a Find and Replace With combination, you would search for the Replace With code, remove it, and place the Find code at that location. To further illustrate these concepts, the following example removes the Search button added to posts in the earlier modification installation exercise.

Time For Action—Uninstalling a Small Modification

1. Locate and open the `templates/subSilver/viewtopic_body.tpl` file of your forum in a text-editing program.

2. Use the text-editing program's search feature to locate this line of text in the file. Again, most programs allow accessing such a feature from their menus or by pressing *Ctrl+F* on Windows systems.

   ```
   //--></script><noscript>{postrow.ICQ_IMG}</noscript>
   {postrow.SEARCH_IMG}</td>
   ```

3. Now, locate the text `{postrow.SEARCH_IMG}` within that line.

4. Delete this text and the single space before it. The line should once again look as it originally did:

   ```
   //--></script><noscript>{postrow.ICQ_IMG}</noscript></td>
   ```

5. Save and close the file. If necessary, upload it to your website, replacing the existing file there. You may repeat all of these steps with the `templates/subBook/viewtopic_body.tpl` file, if you wish.

6. Go to your forum and look at any post. You should see that the Search image is no longer shown.

What Just Happened?

By reversing the actions you took to install the Search button modification, you have removed it from your forum. Instead of finding the original code and adding to it, you searched for the modified code. Then you removed the extra code added by the original modification. This restored the altered file to its original state.

Removing Other Changes

The need to remove new files and database changes is common to both methods of removing file changes reviewed before the previous example. New files added by a modification are quick and easy to deal with: just delete them. Removing database changes is a more complex aspect of uninstallation; however, phpMyAdmin is a handy tool for making this simple. When a modification has added a new table or a new column in a table, you can locate this addition in phpMyAdmin and click a Delete link, which often takes the form of a trash can icon, next to it. phpMyAdmin will ask you to confirm the deletion (or dropping, as it is called when dealing with tables or columns); do so and the change will be gone.

Example Modifications

Thousands of modifications for phpBB have been released for public use in the years since phpBB first appeared. Think of almost any feature you might like to add to or remove from a phpBB forum, and there will probably be at least one modification for that already. New modifications are created and released each week so the possibilities for customizing a forum through this method are endless.

One of the most popular modifications is the massive **File Attachment Mod**, which contains over 140 files. It adds a new feature to phpBB's posting forums allowing users to upload files that will be attached to and displayed with their posts. Another commonly used example is Modify Profile, formerly known as Add New Field to Profile. This modification is an instruction guide for adding new information fields to user registration and profile-editing forms. Many different kinds of fields can be added, ranging from simple text entry boxes to drop-down selection lists. The data stored in the new field can also be displayed in public profiles, topics, posts, and other places throughout a forum. Dozens of modifications alter or add new BBCodes. User and administration management tools, online games, stores, chat rooms, recent topics, download systems, phpBB bug fixes or upgrades, and website portals are examples of some other widely used modifications.

These lists are only scratching the surface when it comes to describing the types of modifications available for your use. It will definitely be worth your time to check out a few websites that list modifications; you will find something that you want to install at your forum if you look closely enough. Chances are you will find many things to use in customizing your forum.

Moving Elements

Some layout alterations can be made to your forum without taking the time to search for a detailed modification. While you can find modification downloads for some of these, modifications often don't deal with layout issues very well. The differences in templates, and sometimes those created by other modifications, often force forum administrators to rearrange their layout without any help. In order to move elements like this, you will need to have at least a basic knowledge of HTML coding.

You might have noticed that subSilver and subBook have some statistical data and a login box at the bottom of their forum index pages. One popular change that you can make is to move one or more of those elements to another part of the page. By finding the layout code that creates them in `index_body.tpl` and placing it closer to the top of the file, you can emphasize that your users should log in or the number of users and posts on your forum.

Adding New Elements to Your Forum

Creating new areas in your forum will usually require a full modification, complete with instructions. There are a couple of simple things that can be done without a modification, however. One of these is to add a new link to your forum's header menu.

Time For Action—Adding a Menu Link

1. Locate and open the `templates/subBook/overall_header.tpl` file for editing. You can use the `subSilver` `overall_header.tpl` file instead, if you like.

2. Find the line in this file containing the code `<!-- BEGIN switch_user_logged_out -->`. There will be several tab spaces at the beginning of the line.

3. Insert the following code on a new line before the code you just located:
   ```
    <a href="{U_VIEWONLINE}" class="mainmenu"><img
   src="templates/subBook/images/icon_mini_members.gif" width="12"
   height="13" border="0" alt="{L_WHO_IS_ONLINE}" hspace="3"
   />{L_WHO_IS_ONLINE}</a></span> 
   ```

4. Save your changes to the file and view your forum. You may need to reload or refresh the forum page, but you should see a new Who is Online link with the other links near the top of the forum.

What Just Happened?

The menu links of your forum, like Profile, FAQ, and Search, are created by HTML stored in the `overall_header.tpl` template file. By duplicating a line or series of lines that creates one of these links and altering the line a little, you can create a new menu link. In this case, the new link points to the `viewonline.php` file, which displays a list of users currently visiting the forum. If these steps were written up as a modification, they might look like this:

```
#
#-----[ OPEN ]-------------------------------------
#
templates/subBook/overall_header.tpl
#
#-----[ FIND ]-------------------------------------
#
<!-- BEGIN switch_user_logged_out -->
 <a href="{U_REGISTER}" class="mainmenu"><img
src="templates/subBook/images/icon_mini_register.gif" width="12"
height="13" border="0" alt="{L_REGISTER}" hspace="3"
/>{L_REGISTER}</a></span> 
<!-- END switch_user_logged_out -->
#
#-----[ BEFORE, ADD ]------------------------------
#
 <a href="{U_VIEWONLINE}" class="mainmenu"><img
src="templates/subBook/images/icon_mini_members.gif" width="12"
```

```
height="13" border="0" alt="{L_WHO_IS_ONLINE}" hspace="3"
/>{L_WHO_IS_ONLINE}</a>
</span> 
#
#-----[ SAVE/CLOSE ALL FILES ]----------------------------------------
---
#
# End
```

Adding New Languages

Another common change made by forum administrators is the installation of new
language files. If you plan to have many visitors who are fluent in languages other than
English or cannot read English, you might want to download and install a language pack
from phpBB.com's Downloads section. Each language pack adds a new option to the
Board Language drop-down list in user profiles and the Administration Control Panel.
Selecting that option will cause the forum to be displayed in that language. Posts will not
be translated, but many links and other default text will.

When adding language packs, you should keep in mind that you may have to edit the new
language files. Some modifications will include new language files or instructions for
editing language files. If you add a new language and do not copy these changes to that
language, then some text will not appear on your forum. This situation is similar to that
for modifications and templates; you must edit every language, even if the modification's
instructions only mention one.

Summary

phpBB is excellent and powerful forum software in many areas. Customization
possibilities are one of the strongest. With the skills and knowledge you've gained in this
chapter, you can give your forum a complete face-lift or expand its features beyond
anything you might have imagined. Specifically, you learned:

- A phpBB style creates the appearance of a forum
- Editing a style's components allows you to change any aspect of
  the appearance
- Modifications are instructions for changing phpBB's features,
  and usually have a special format
- How to install and remove styles and modifications downloaded
  from websites
- Methods of editing any of phpBB's files and solving errors

6
Forum Administration

In the previous chapters you've read about how your board works and how to customize the way it looks. Some advanced topics were skipped so that you could concentrate on the most important and widely used phpBB features. It's now time to master phpBB, and go through details that will make you a real power-phpBB-admin.

In this chapter you'll learn about:

- Making your board multi-lingual
- Configuring avatars
- Managing smilies
- Assigning ranks
- Forum permissions
- User permissions
- Usergroups and group permissions
- Database backups and restore—a second look
- The human side—moderators, flamewars, and banning

Making Your Board Multi-Lingual

phpBB is developed to support multiple languages in the same board. The whole interface (screens, messages, buttons, emails, and so on) is translated into more than 50 languages. The translators are not members of the phpBB team, but are native-speaking volunteers, and this guarantees that the translations are correct and ready to be installed on your board. Thus, you provide a better service for your community, giving them an interface they feel more comfortable with.

Time For Action—Adding Spanish Support to Your Forum

1. Go to the phpBB.com downloads page
   `http://www.phpbb.com/downloads.php`.

2. Scroll down to the Language & Image Packs section and locate the Español
   (Spanish) row:

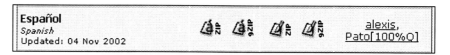

3. Choose your preferred compression type—ZIP or GZIP—and download the
   two archives in the selected format. Let's choose the ZIP format as an
   example. The first ZIP file contains the texts for the phpBB interfaces, and
   the second one contains the interface graphics, such as the buttons for a new
   post, quote, and so on. These graphics are provided for the default subSilver
   theme only.

4. Uncompress the first file, `lang_spanish.zip` (and FTP it if you're using a
   hosted service), into the `language` directory within your phpBB directory.
   This should create a `lang_spanish` subdirectory under `language`.

5. Uncompress the second file, `subsilver_spanish.zip`, to a selected
   directory. When you do this, you'll notice that it has a nested directory
   structure, and in your selected directory, you'll have a
   `subSilver/images/lang_spanish` path.
   If you follow this path, you'll find a number of GIF files.

6. Copy (and/or FTP) the last directory (`lang_spanish`, the one that contains
   all the GIF files) into your corresponding phpBB directory,
   `templates/subSilver/images`.

What Just Happened?

After you have successfully uncompressed the ZIP archives and copied their content,
your forum structure will look like the following screenshot:

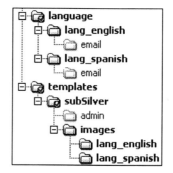

Now if you log in to your forum and access your profile, you'll see that the Board Language dropdown now has two values, as shown in the illustration:

If you change your preference to Spanish, you'll see the whole board with a Spanish interface. ¡Hola!

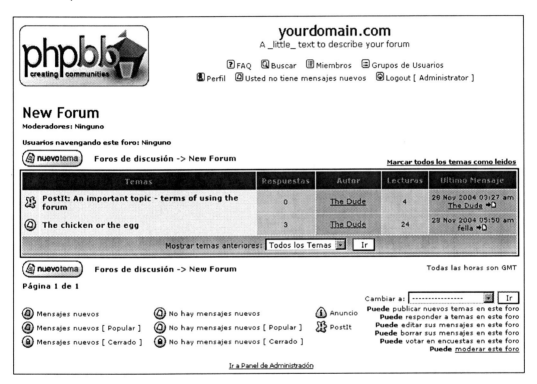

Now you have two languages installed, but English is still the default language for the board. If your community is mainly Spanish speaking, you can consider changing the default language. To do that you need to go to the Administration Panel and follow the Configuration link under General Admin.

Avatars: Enabling and Configuring

Avatars are those small images that reside under the username in all postings and are also displayed when viewing a user's profile. They are not enabled by default in phpBB, but can be enabled pretty easily using the Administrator Panel.

There are three options for the use of avatars, and they are not exclusive; you can select any number of them.

- Option one is to enable the so-called **gallery avatars**: The images that can be used as avatars are selected by you and hosted on the same server on which phpBB runs. Users can select their preferred avatar only from the offered images.

- Option two is to enable **remote avatars**: The avatar image can reside on any server on the Internet and the users are just linking to it, using image's URL address (starting with http://).

- Option three is to allow users to **upload avatars**: The users copy their images to your server, and phpBB reads them from there when displaying a post.

All these options have pros and cons to consider when making a decision.

- **Remote avatars** are your safest bet in terms of server security; it's all in the hands of the users, and your board is not responsible for hosting or managing the images. However, some users may want to use images that are on their hard drives and are nowhere to be found on the Internet. Also, because of the dynamic nature of the Internet, many pages and even whole sites appear and disappear in a single day. This means that an image your user selected today may not be available tomorrow, and some browsers (like Internet Explorer) will display a broken image icon instead, which is not pretty. Or even if an avatar is available but hosted on a slow site, it may slow the whole page down. There may be issues when the board members use avatars hosted on servers that don't allow hotlinking. Moreover, you don't have control over the sizes of the avatars. Somebody can put a real big picture as an avatar and ruin the whole look of a topic.

- With **gallery avatars**, you have control over the size of the images, because you're the one selecting them. The drawbacks are that these images will increase your bandwidth usage and will be too restrictive for the users, as they can only pick an image from pre-defined choices.

- **Uploaded avatars** can lead to increased bandwidth, which can be an issue for heavily used boards with a lot of users. Another issue might be that some hosts may not allow you to use file uploads, because of the general concern that anything that a user does to a server can be potentially dangerous. Apart from that, uploaded avatars have quite a few benefits, like defining the size in pixels and the disk size in bytes for the images. With the uploaded avatars, users are free to use any possible image they can lay their hands on, not only those images available on the Internet.

To configure the avatars, you need to log in as an administrator, go to the Administrator Panel, and bring up the general configuration form:

Here's what the avatars section in the configuration form looks like:

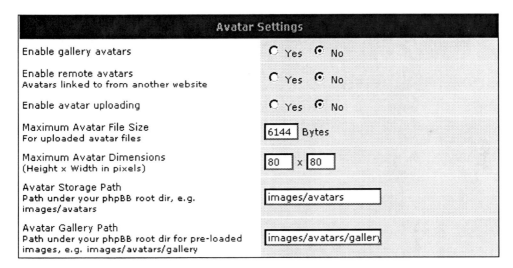

The first three fields represent the three avatar options discussed. The next three fields are applicable to uploaded avatars only, and the very last field is for gallery avatars only.

To feel more comfortable with the avatar options, the best thing to do is just to enable all three options and play around with the avatars. After that, you can make your choice.

Getting gallery avatars

You can get avatars for your gallery from http://www.phpbb.com/styles/. Click on Downloads, and then Avatars. Unzip the packages into a subfolder within the avatars directory you specified in the configuration (the default is images/avatars/gallery).

Don't forget permissions

If you enable avatar uploads, you have to make sure the directory specified to contain the images (the default is images/avatars) is writable, meaning chmod 777 for Linux systems. Setting file permissions was explained in Chapter 2.

You can have categories of gallery avatars; actually you have to have at least one category. What does this mean? It means that you have to copy *all* your gallery avatars into sub-directories of the main avatar gallery directory. For example, you'd copy dog.gif and cat.gif to images/avatars/gallery/pets, even if you host a pet-lovers site and pets would be the only gallery you'll ever need. In any event, this feature helps you keep your galleries organized.

Managing Smilies

phpBB comes with a default set of smilies, but you can change the defaults or add new ones. In fact, your users may request that you add more smilies, because the defaults may not be enough for them to express their emotions. Or it's just that some of your members may be used to seeing different smilies in other boards that they visit, and miss those cute graphics in your board.

As you know already, **smilies** and **emoticons** are synonyms. "Smilies" is a more widespread term, while "emoticons" is probably more accurate, because not all of the small round faces are smiling. One other interesting thing is that the word "smilie" can be spelled as "smilie" *and* "smiley". phpBB prefers "smiley" but a Google search returned more results on "smilie", so it's apparently more often used. In this book, we've adopted "smilie".

phpBB gives you the ability to:

- Edit or delete an existing smilie
- Add new smilies one by one
- Add new smilies in batches using the special .pak files

- Create .pak files using your currently installed smilies; this is a good idea if you have created a number of smilies that you'd like to share with other phpBB administrators.

Smilies' Properties

Let's first see what a smilie consists of. Every smilie has:

- **An image**: Smilie images like ☺ and ☺ reside in the images/smilies directory of your board's directory structure.

- **A code**: The code is the sequence of characters a poster needs to type (or have them typed automatically by clicking the corresponding image) in order to display the selected smilie in a post. For the example icons in the previous bullet, the corresponding codes are :D and :?. Sometimes there can be several codes for one emoticon, and so there are several ways to include the same image in a post. You can use :D or :-D or :grin:, and the result will always be the ☺ image.

- **An emotion**: This is a human-readable representation of the smilie. It may be displayed (depending on the browser) as a tool-tip when a reader holds the mouse over a poster's emoticon (in HTML terms, it is the alt attribute of the img tag).

Here's a pair of images showing an example. The left-hand illustration shows a posting at the moment of writing; the right-hand one shows how the posting is displayed (with the mouse over the smilie) in an Internet Explorer browser window:

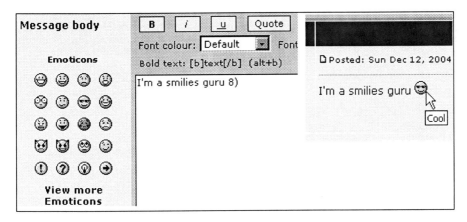

Smilies Administration Panel

All smilie operations are accessible through the Administration Panel using the Smilies link under the General Admin section:

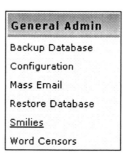

Clicking this link brings up a list of existing smilies:

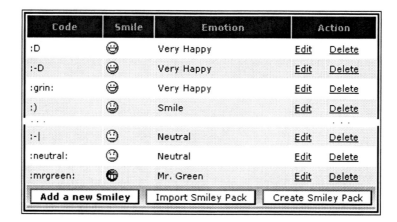

This illustration shows the listing cut down in the middle. The listing can grow pretty long as you add new smilies. You can see all the properties of the smilies—the code, the image, and the emotion they represent—as well as the possible actions that you can execute on them.

Before proceeding with the following exercises, it may be a good idea to make a backup of your images/smilies directory, just in case you want to revert to the default smilies.

Editing or Deleting a Smilie

To edit or delete a smilie, use the appropriate link next to the smilie in question.

Be careful when playing around, because when you click Delete, there will be no "Are you sure?" confirmation; the smilie will be removed permanently. Deleting a smilie means that it can no longer be used in postings; it also means that any older postings that use this emoticon will display the code, but not the image.

Deleting a smilie doesn't delete the actual image from the server, as chances are this image may be used for other smilies as well. For example, if you delete the smilie with the :-D code, the 😄 image won't be deleted, because it's also used for the :D smilie. Even if you delete all smilies that use a certain image, the image will stay on the server and can be used later on, by defining a new smilie.

To edit a smilie, use the Edit link next to it. This brings up a form with all the smilie properties, as shown on the illustration.

The Smilie Image File drop-down field lists all the files found in the images/smilies folder of your board installation. Selecting an image file from the dropdown displays this image next to the dropdown.

Adding New Smilies

The simplest way to add a new smilie is by using an existing image.

Time For Action—Adding a New Smilie Using an Existing Image

1. In the smilies admin panel, click the Add a new Smiley button. The same form as the one for editing is displayed.
2. In the first field, type :mg:.
3. In the second field (dropdown), select icon_mrgreen.gif.
4. In the last field, type Mr. Green.
5. Click Submit.

What Just Happened?

You created a new Mr. Green smilie using the same existing image. In other words, you defined a new way for the users to use this emoticon. Now the users can have Mr. Green displayed in their postings in two ways: by using either the default code, :mrgreen:, or the new one, :mg:.

Now let's add a completely new smilie. Let's say you took Mr. Green's icon and painted it all orange. Now let's call this guy Mr. Orange 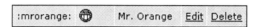 and name the file `mr_orange.gif`.

Time For Action—Adding a Custom Smilie

1. Copy/FTP the `mr_orange.gif` file to your `images/smilies` directory.
2. Go to the smilies admin panel and click the Add a new Smiley button.
3. In the first field, type :mrorange:.
4. In the second field select mr_orange.gif.
5. In the last field, type Mr. Orange.
6. Click Submit.

What Just Happened?

You've just added a brand new shiny smilie face to your board. You can see it now in the smilies listing.

Adding Smilies with a .pak File

You may be wondering how to create GIF files like the one used in the example above. Well, this is a topic that is outside the scope of the book, but you can find many tools and tutorials on the Internet. If you don't want to deal with the graphics, don't worry; there is good news for you. There are lots of smilie images out there on the Web, available for you do download and use in your board. To ease the installation, phpBB has a feature to add smilies in batches using the `.pak` files. This "pak" stands for "package".

If you visit `http://www.phpbb.com/styles`, click on Downloads, and then Smilies, you'll see a listing of smilie packages for you to choose from. Let's pick one of those packages to download, the one called More smilies.

If you download `eusasmiles.zip` and uncompress it, you'll see that it contains a number of GIF files and one `eusa.pak` file. Don't be scared by the unknown extension of this file, it's just a plain text file. If you open it with any text-editing program (like Notepad or WordPad for Windows) and look at the file contents, you'll notice that it contains simply the smilie properties, divided by the sequence of characters `=+:`, used as a delimiter.

The last line of the file, for example, says:

```
eusa_silenced.gif=+:Silenced=+::-#
```

What this means is that `:-#` is the code for an emoticon that means Silenced and whose icon image is called `eusa_silenced.gif`.

Now let's use the provided `.pak` file to quickly add a bunch of new smilies to the board.

Time For Action—Adding Smilies Using a .pak File

1. Copy the uncompressed content (the GIF images and the `.pak` file) to the `images/smilies` directory of your bulletin board.
2. Go to the smilies admin area in the Administration Panel and click on the Import Smiley Pack button. You'll see the Smiley Pack Import form.

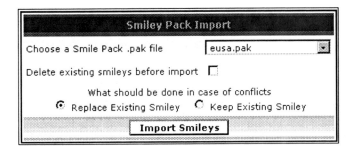

3. In the dropdown, choose eusa.pak.
4. Leave the other fields as they are. They represent your options of what to do with the existing smilies and how to handle conflicts, if any.
5. Click Import Smileys.

What Just Happened?

You've added a whole lot of new smilies in a single shot. You can see them now in the smilies listing, right after the Mr. Orange smiley you added in the previous exercise. Here's a part of what the new smilies listing will look like:

:mrorange:		Mr. Orange	Edit	Delete
=D>		Applause	Edit	Delete
#-o		d'oh!	Edit	Delete
=P~		Drool	Edit	Delete
:^o		Liar	Edit	Delete

Creating a .pak File

You can create a .pak file with your existing smilies configuration. You can use it for backup purposes or to share your icons. Let's say you've created not only Mr. Orange, but also Mr. White, Mr. Pink, Mr. Brown, and Mr. Blonde, and have added them by hand following the same procedure as for Mr. Orange.

:mrwhite:		Mr. White
:mrpink:		Mr. Pink
:mrbrown:		Mr. Brown
:mrblonde:		Mr. Blonde

Now let's create a .pak file that will contain the properties of all smilies you've added, so that you can share your smilies with other phpBB administrators.

> The images used in this chapter are available in the book's code download at
> http://www.packtpub.com.

Time For Action—Creating a .pak File

1. Go to the smilies admin and click the Create Smiley Pack button.

2. You get information about working with .pak files and an option to download the .pak file generated for you. Download it. The file is called smilies.pak by default, but you can always change its name to something else, like reservoir_dogs.pak for example.

3. The package file contains *all* the properties for all the smilies on your board, but you actually need only your *five* custom ones. So open the .pak file in a text editor and remove all unnecessary lines, leaving just your five lines. The .pak file contents now should look like:

```
mr_orange.gif=+:Mr. Orange=+::mrorange:
mr_white.gif=+:Mr. White=+::mrwhite:
mr_pink.gif=+:Mr. Pink=+::mrpink:
mr_brown.gif=+:Mr. Brown=+::mrbrown:
mr_blonde.gif=+:Mr. Blonde=+::mrblonde:
```

4. Zip this .pak file together with the five images.

What Just Happened?

You've created a .pak file containing all the smilies you've created. You can send it to other phpBB admins if they want to install your custom smilies.

Assigning Ranks

Ranks are another way of giving your community members a credit for their participation. Only one rank exists by default: the Site Admin rank. There are two types of ranks that you can create: **ranks by number of posts** and **special ranks**. The first type of ranks are automatic, and are assigned as a member keeps posting. The second type are not dependent on the number of posts, and you can assign them as you may find appropriate, using the user management facility in the Administration Panel.

Ranks are given names, typically something like New user, Enthusiast, Forum addict, and so on. Ranks can optionally have rank images. When viewing postings by a user, the name of the rank assigned to the user is displayed under the username, and the rank image is displayed under the rank name, above the avatar. Here's an example of how the author-info area of a posting looks when a rank is assigned:

In this illustration, The Dude is the username you already know from the previous chapters, Forum Wizard is the rank name, the five stars is the rank image, and the paintbrush daub is the user's avatar.

The following examples will help you get some hands-on experience on assigning ranks. For the sake of the first example, let's assume that you have created five rank images. The images are in GIF format and show one, two, three, four, and five blue stars respectively, like this:

- rank1.gif: ★
- rank2.gif: ★★
- rank3.gif: ★★★
- rank4.gif: ★★★★
- rank5.gif: ★★★★★

If creating GIF files is not your cup of tea, don't worry, you can download rank images from the Internet: one place to look is, of course, the phpBB.com site. Visit the styles section and click on Downloads followed by Rank Images. You can also find many rank images on the phpBBHacks site, at http://www.phpbbhacks.com/rankimages.php.

Time For Action—Creating Automatic Ranks

1. In the images directory of your board, create a subdirectory called ranks. This will keep rank-related images separate from the rest of the images.

2. Copy the files listed above (rank1.gif through to rank5.gif) to the newly created directory.

3. In the Administration Panel, click the Ranks link (the last link in the administration menu).

4. Click the Add new rank button.

5. You're presented with the Rank Administration form. Fill it out as shown on the illustration:

6. Click Submit.

7. Repeat steps 4 through 6 until you use all rank images. At the end you'll have your ranks setup as the following:

Rank Title	Minimum Posts	Set as Special Rank	Edit	Delete
Site Admin	-	Yes	Edit	Delete
Newbie	1	No	Edit	Delete
Oldie	5	No	Edit	Delete
Zealot	10	No	Edit	Delete
Guru	20	No	Edit	Delete
Forum Wizard	30	No	Edit	Delete
		Add new rank		

What Just Happened?

You've successfully set up an automated ranking system that will display a rank name and a rank image after each member's username in the member's postings. The exact rank will be determined by phpBB based on the total number of posts by this member.

In practice of course you'd want to use a much bigger number of postings, but for testing the functionality this is enough.

Now let's take a look at the procedure for creating special ranks and how you can assign a special rank to the members you feel are special.

Time For Action—Creating and Assigning a Special Rank

1. In the ranks listing click Add new rank.
2. Fill out the form as shown:

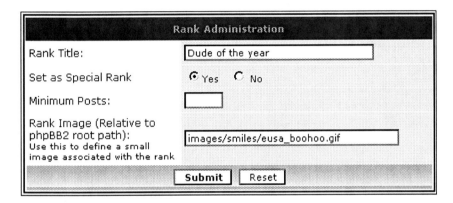

3. Click Submit.
4. Now in the left menu, click the Management link in the User Admin section.
5. In the text field, type The Dude and click Look up user.
6. Scroll down to the bottom of the user admin form. In the Rank Title dropdown, select Dude of the year.
7. Click Submit.

What Just Happened?

Steps 1-3: You created a special rank, meaning that it's not related to the number of postings. The Minimum Posts field was left blank, as it's not applicable to special ranks. Actually, even if you do enter something in it, the value will be ignored by phpBB. In this example you didn't create a new rank image, but reused an existing smilie image instead.

Steps 4-7: You assigned the newly created special rank to a user. If you now visit the front end of your board and find a posting by The Dude, you'll see the new rank.

Understanding Forum Permissions

Forum permissions were discussed in Chapter 4, but we'll now take a more insightful approach so that we'll be able to specify more precisely who can do what on your board.

Let's start with defining two important terms: **permission types** and **permission levels**.

Permission Types and Permission Levels

Permission types and **permission levels** are two important terms when dealing with phpBB permissions, and understanding these will help you when you think of how to assign and control privileges:

- **Permission types** are the actions that a user can do in the board, such as view, reply, vote, etc. When you think about permission types, think *what*, as in "What can be done?"

- **Permission levels** reflect restrictions about who can do a certain actions. Every user has at least one permission level. When you think about permission levels, think *who* as in "Who can do it?"

The following list discusses the permission types ("*What-s*") that exist, and the capabilities they provide to a user. (You already know what these actions mean, as they were described in detail in the previous chapters.)

- **View**: The user can see that a forum exists on the board front page.

- **Read**: The user can list forum topics, read the postings, view the members' profiles, and their contact info.

- **Reply**: The user can post in existing topics.

- **Post**: The user can start new topics.

- **Edit**: The user can edit their own postings.

- **Delete**: The user can delete his or her own postings, provided no one has replied to them.

- **Sticky**: The user can start sticky topics. This is dependent on the post privilege—if you cannot post, you certainly cannot post sticky topics.

- **Announce**: The user can start announcements. Just like the sticky type, the post privilege is a prerequisite.

- **Vote**: The user can vote in polls.

- **Poll create**: The user can create polls for others to vote in.

Permission levels, or "*Who-s*", can also be thought of as user types. Here are the possible permission levels:

- **ALL**: Everybody who accesses the board; this includes members who are currently not logged in.

- **REG**: A member registered at the board and currently logged in.

- **PRIVATE**: A special permission level that is assigned individually. In order for a user on this level to communicate in privacy with others, this user has to be given private access to a private forum. This is the trickiest part of the permissions, so don't be scared if you don't understand it yet. There will be some examples to clarify this concept.

- **MOD**: A moderator who can do everything to a forum.

- **ADMIN**: A board administrator (someone like you, who can access the Administration Panel).

Simple and Advanced Mode of Setting Permissions

As you know already, there are two ways of setting permissions: simple mode and advanced mode. The simple mode has been discussed in Chapter 4, and as you know, it gives you predefined permissions options.

If you access the advanced mode, you'll see all the possible permissions types and permission levels we discussed above. To do that, log in as an administrator, go to the Administrator Panel, under Forum Admin section click Permissions, look up any forum, and click Advanced Mode. Here's what you'll see:

This screen shows all the permission types (displayed as table headers) and the permission levels (these are the values in the drop-down boxes). The advanced permissions shown in the above illustration would be displayed in simple mode as Registered, shown in the following illustration:

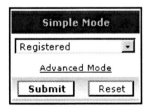

We have seen that the simple modes are a quicker and easier way of setting permissions. Let's now find out exactly *what* the simple modes— Public, Registered, Private, and Moderators—mean, and *which* advanced permissions settings they group together.

A rough idea about these modes is that they define who can post in the selected forum (for example, everybody can post in Public forums, but only logged-in members can post in Registered forums, and so on).

Except for the Public mode, all other simple modes have an option that includes [Hidden] in the name. This means that the users without sufficient privileges are unable to not just *post*, but even to *see* that such forums exist.

Here's a more detailed explanation of the simple mode permissions:

- Public: Everybody (permission level ALL) can see the public forum, read it, reply in topics, and start new topics. Registered and logged-in members (permission level REG) can even edit and delete their own postings, vote, and create polls.

- Registered: ALL can see and read the forum. REG can post, start topics, edit and delete their own postings, vote, and start polls.

- Registered [Hidden]: Same as above, except that ALL can no longer see nor read the forum—they have to register to be able to do so.

- Private: The forum is visible to ALL just to see it exists, but is PRIVATE, and only users who are explicitly allowed access to this forum can read postings, post, start topics, edit and delete their own postings, and start and vote for polls. The next two sections of this chapter explain how to grant private access to users. Another specific thing about private forums is that the private members can also post sticky postings. Announcements, however, are still a "moderators-only" area.

- Private [Hidden]: Same as above, except that ALL can no longer see that this forum exists. It's a really protected and private forum.

- Moderators: same as Registered and Private, but only moderators can read, post, start topics, vote, and so on. A user has to be a moderator in this forum in order to use it. Being a moderator for any other forum doesn't mean the user can access this one.

- Moderators [Hidden]: Same as above except that ALL can't even see that such a forum exists.

The following table explains the same as the bullets point above, but in greater detail. You'll see that it is actually a pretty good way to understand permissions in general.

x	Public	Registered	Registered [Hidden]	Private	Private [Hidden]	Moderators	Moderators [Hidden]
View	ALL	ALL	REG	ALL	PRIVATE	ALL	MOD
Read	ALL	ALL	REG	PRIVATE	PRIVATE	MOD	MOD
Post	ALL	REG	REG	PRIVATE	PRIVATE	MOD	MOD
Reply	ALL	REG	REG	PRIVATE	PRIVATE	MOD	MOD
Edit	REG	REG	REG	PRIVATE	PRIVATE	MOD	MOD
Delete	REG	REG	REG	PRIVATE	PRIVATE	MOD	MOD
Sticky	MOD	MOD	MOD	PRIVATE	PRIVATE	MOD	MOD
Announcement	MOD	MOD	MOD	MOD	MOD	MOD	MOD
Vote	REG	REG	REG	PRIVATE	PRIVATE	MOD	MOD
Poll create	REG	REG	REG	PRIVATE	PRIVATE	MOD	MOD

When setting permissions it's always a good idea to choose one of the simple modes. They have been carefully selected by the phpBB team to match the most-used forum types. If you feel you need something different, you can always switch to advanced mode. In such a case, it's a good idea to first use a simple mode to set and save permissions, and then edit them again, and switch to advanced mode for fine-tuning.

Time For Action—Creating and Fine-Tuning a Private Forum

1. Log in as an administrator and go to the Administrator Panel.
2. Go to Management under Forum Admin.
3. Create a new category called Special forums, and then a new forum called The Dudes forum in this category.
4. Click on the Permissions link under Forum Admin.
5. Select The Dudes forum from the Select a Forum dropdown and click Look up Forum.
6. You are now in the Forum Permission Control area and Simple Mode.
7. Select Private [Hidden] and click Submit.
8. Repeat step 5.
9. Click Advanced Mode to switch to a more powerful editing form.
10. In the Sticky column, change the PRIVATE value to MOD.
11. Click Submit to save the settings.

What Just Happened

Steps 1-3: You've created a new category and a new forum.

Steps 4-7: You've set the forum permissions using the simple mode. You've set the permissions so that only special private members can see, read, post, etc., on the forum. The only thing private members cannot do is post announcements. (Of course if the users are not moderators, they can only edit or delete *their* postings, and not other private members' postings.)

Steps 8-11: You've set the permissions again, this time using advanced mode, and disallowed private members to post sticky posts.

Now if you visit the front page of your board, you'll see the new category and the new forum (because you're logged in as an administrator, and can see and do everything), but as soon as you log out, the forum and the whole category will no longer be visible.

In the next two sections we'll find out how to make a private forum visible for some members by making them private members.

Understanding User Permissions

You already know how to use the permissions area of the Administrator Panel to make a user a moderator; let's look at what *else* you can do. If you remember, user permissions are accessible through the Permissions link under the User Admin section:

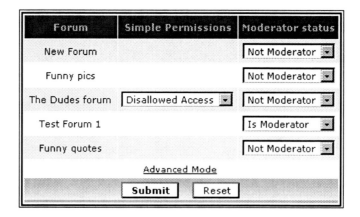

You see that along with setting the moderator status here, you can also specify user permissions for each forum (in other words, specify forum permissions that apply to a specific user only). Note that you can use this option only for *private forums*; for all other types of forums, the forum permissions are applied and the user permissions cannot override them.

146

A *private forum* by definition has at least one permission type set to PRIVATE.

In the previous section, we created The Dudes forum as a private forum, so now in the user permission control area, we can allow or disallow a user from accessing the private forum. Allowing access means that this user becomes a private member and can do whatever private members are allowed to do—the user will have the permission types (for example read, post, etc.) that were set for the PRIVATE level in the forum's administration.

Time For Action—Making The Dude a Private User of The Dudes Forum

1. Log in as an administrator and go to the Administration Panel.
2. Select Permissions under User Admin.
3. Type The Dude and click Look up User. At this point, you see something similar to the previous illustration (at the beginning of this section).
4. On The Dudes forum row, change the first dropdown from Disallowed Access to Allowed Access.
5. Click Submit to save the permission settings.

What Just Happened?

You've allowed The Dude to access the private The Dudes forum. By doing this, you've made The Dude a private member of this forum and let him enjoy all the permission types that were set to PRIVATE on the forum's admin.

If you repeat steps 1-4 again and then click Advanced Mode, you'll see a screen like the following:

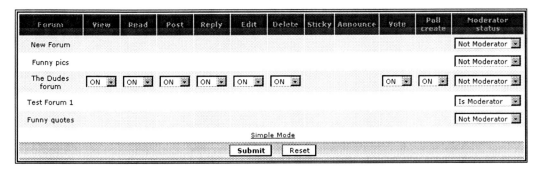

This Advanced Mode form allows you to be even more precise on per-user basis by turning off some permission types that are allowed by default for private members. You don't have options in the Sticky and Announce columns, because these permission types were set to MOD and not PRIVATE when setting up the forum permissions.

There is another way of restricting user privileges, and it has nothing to do with the permissions—the ability to allow or deny private messages and avatars on a per-user basis as well as to activate or deactivate a user. This can be done by editing a user's profile in the Administrator Panel (the Management link under User Admin section) and using the Special admin-only fields, shown in the following illustration:

Special admin-only fields	
These fields are not able to be modified by the users. Here you can set their status and other options that are not given to users.	
User is active	⦿ Yes ○ No
Can send Private Messages	○ Yes ⦿ No
Can display avatar	⦿ Yes ○ No

Usergroups and Group Permissions

Usergroups are a way for you to create groups of users, based on some criteria that you find appropriate. You don't have to use usergroups—in the default phpBB installation, no groups exist—but this can be a useful feature.

Users access the usergroups by using the Usergroups ⊞ Usergroups top navigation menu icon. You as an administrator can also use this link; it gives you some administrative options as well. When accessed by a group moderator, this link also brings up the interface for moderating a group.

Every group has a moderator. This community member is responsible for managing the group, and is not to be confused with a forum moderator. Group moderators have no special privileges over the forum topics or postings; they have special privileges only for the group they are moderating. They can add and remove members from the group, can accept or deny membership applications and can change a group type.

What types of groups exist? A group can be open, closed, or hidden.

- An **open** group is visible for everybody and accepts new members. In order to become a member to the group, a user applies to join. The group moderator can accept or deny applications. He or she can also add members to the group without having those members to apply first.

- A **closed** group is a group that does not accept applications. The group moderator can still add new members.

- A **hidden** group is like the closed group, but is not displayed to the users. Only logged-in members of the group can see it. The group moderator adds new members.

Time For Action—Creating a New Group

1. Log in as an administrator and go to the Administration Panel.
2. Click on the Management link under the Group Admin menu section:

3. Click the Create New Group button.
4. Fill out the form as shown:

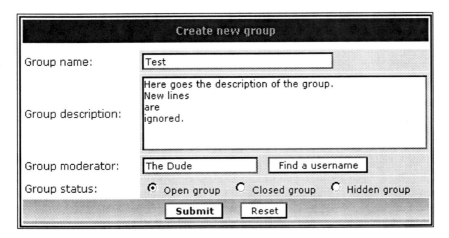

5. Click Submit.

What Just Happened?

You've successfully created a new usergroup called Test with the world-famous user The Dude as a moderator. This group is open and accepts membership applications.

If you now visit the front end of the board, go to Usergroups, and view the information about the Test group, you'll see a screen like the following:

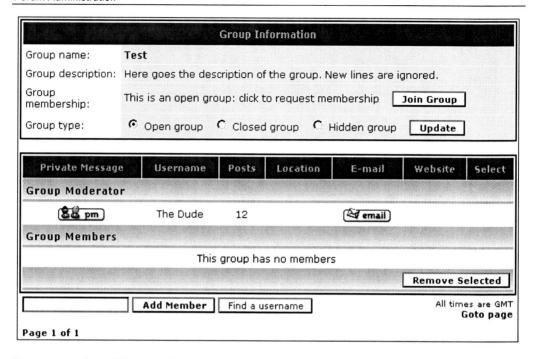

Because you're still logged in as an administrator, you see the group moderator options for changing the group type and adding/removing members. You don't see the membership applications interface, because no applications currently exist. Also, because you are not a member of this open group, you see the Join Group button.

Click the Join Group button to apply for a group membership. This sends the group moderator an email advising that there is a new pending application. The moderator logs in, goes to the usergroup (the screen above), and accepts or denies this application. If the application is accepted, you become a member of the group and get an email communicating that fact.

Time For Action—Editing a Group

1. You're still logged in as an administrator; go to the Administration Panel.
2. Under Group Admin, click Management.
3. The Test group is selected; click on Look up group.

4. Change the name and the description of the group as shown. Also, change the Group status to Hidden group.

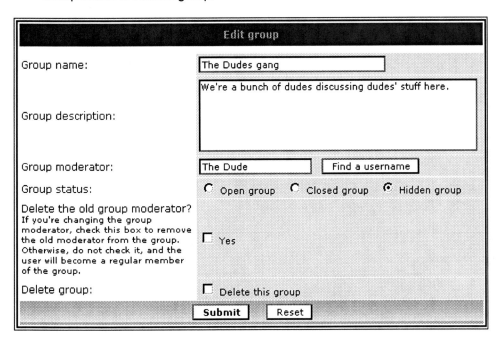

5. Click on Submit to save the changes.

What Just Happened?

You have successfully edited the group. It was a simple thing to do, just like creating the group. But this time you had two additional checkboxes on the Edit group form: you could delete the group, and when changing the group moderator, you could select whether the group's ex-mod stays in the group as a regular member or is removed from the group.

Group Permissions

The administrator has the option of setting group permissions. The group moderator doesn't have control over them. The group permissions work just like the user permissions. The only difference is that you can set a permission type once per group and it will apply to all members of the group. This can save you a lot of work. Although a member is part of a group and has group permissions, you can still override these permissions on a per-user basis. This means, for example, that you can specify that all members of a usergroup can post announcements, but then forbid this for a specific user of the group.

Group permissions are accessible through the Permissions link in the Group Admin section of the Administration Panel navigation menu:

One common task you might want to do is to create a special hidden forum that can be used only by certain users (for example, a forum for moderators, where they can talk about board or user-related issues without those discussions being publicly available).

In order to do this:

- Create a Private [Hidden] forum.
- Create a private group.
- Give access to the group to use the private forum.

So far we have discussed the first two points. We've created a special private hidden forum called The Dudes forum and you've a hidden group called The Dudes gang. Now the last point: giving The Dudes gang access to The Dudes forum.

Time For Action—Setting Group Permissions

1. Log in as an administrator, and go to the Administration Panel.
2. Select Permissions under the Group Admin section of the navigation menu.
3. In the next screen, select The Dudes gang and click on Look up Group.
4. In the Group Permissions Control form, switch to Advanced Mode.

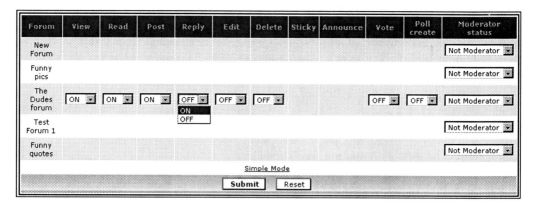

5. Change all dropdowns on The Dudes forum row from OFF to ON.
6. Click Submit to save the permission settings.

What Just Happened?

You've granted privileges for the whole The Dudes gang usergroup to be able to read, post, vote, etc., in The Dudes forum forum. Here are a few more points for you to think about and experiment.

- You can use the Advanced Mode for granting permissions by turning ON/OFF selectively; it's not necessary to turn all ON or all OFF.

- Simple Mode cannot be used for setting group permissions, not in the phpBB version this book is based on.

- Forum moderators and group moderators are completely independent of each other. The Dude is a group moderator of The Dudes gang, but is not a forum moderator in The Dudes forum.

- You can make everybody in a group a moderator by setting the group's Is Moderator status.

- Group permissions are a fast way to set permissions, but you can still use the user permissions to be more specific. User permissions override group permissions.

- You can have several usergroups with different access to a forum. For example, you can set up an open group called "Junior Dudes" that can only *read* The Dudes forum, while the good old The Dudes gang usergroup can still *post*.

Second Look into Database Backups and Restore

You already know how to use phpBB's backup and restore utilities. It was mentioned that they might not work as expected, if you have a very big database and your hosting provider has set some rules on server resources usage. So now let's take a look at using other means of achieving the same result. MySQL is the RDBMS used in this section; it's the most popular to run phpBB on.

Using phpMyAdmin

phpMyAdmin can be used for backing up and restoring you forum database. It has an export utility that can help you create an SQL dump of a table or a database or even *all* the databases on a server. An SQL dump is a text file that contains all the necessary SQL commands needed to create a copy of a table or a database. phpBB's database backup and restore utility uses the same SQL dumps.

If you're feeling nosy you can open an SQL dump with a text editor, and you'll see a whole bunch of SQL commands that start like this:

```
-- phpMyAdmin SQL Dump
-- version 2.6.0-rc2
-- http://www.phpmyadmin.net
--
-- Host: localhost
-- Generation Time: Dec 14, 2004 at 10:45 PM
-- Server version: 3.23.47
-- PHP Version: 4.3.0
--
-- Database: 'forums'
--

-- --------------------------------------------------------

--
-- Table structure for table 'phpbb_auth_access'
--

CREATE TABLE 'phpbb_auth_access' (
  'group_id' mediumint(8) NOT NULL default '0',
  'forum_id' smallint(5) unsigned NOT NULL default '0',
  'auth_view' tinyint(1) NOT NULL default '0',
  'auth_read' tinyint(1) NOT NULL default '0',
  'auth_post' tinyint(1) NOT NULL default '0',
  'auth_reply' tinyint(1) NOT NULL default '0',
  'auth_edit' tinyint(1) NOT NULL default '0',
  'auth_delete' tinyint(1) NOT NULL default '0',
  'auth_sticky' tinyint(1) NOT NULL default '0',
  'auth_announce' tinyint(1) NOT NULL default '0',
  'auth_vote' tinyint(1) NOT NULL default '0',
  'auth_pollcreate' tinyint(1) NOT NULL default '0',
  'auth_attachments' tinyint(1) NOT NULL default '0',
  'auth_mod' tinyint(1) NOT NULL default '0',
  KEY 'group_id' (`group_id`),
  KEY 'forum_id' (`forum_id`)
) TYPE=MyISAM;

--
-- Dumping data for table `phpbb_auth_access`
--
```

If this looks like an alien language to you, don't worry; you don't need to know any of that. It was just an example to give an idea of what SQL dumps look like. The important thing is to know how to create them and use them.

The good thing about phpMyAdmin is that it allows you to create SQL dumps of individual tables, not of the whole database in a single file. This is good—if you need to restore the database later on and your hosting provider has restrictions on the size of the files that you upload, then you may be able to work around the upload limit by splitting a possibly large database into several smaller SQL dumps.

Let's look at an example that will help you understand the procedure of database backups and restoring using phpMyAdmin. For the sake of this and the other examples further in this chapter, let's assume that the database that contains your board is named forums, your database username is dbuser, and your password to access the database is dbpass.

Time For Action—Creating an SQL Database Dump

You are currently on the front page for your "forums" database. It looks like the following illustration:

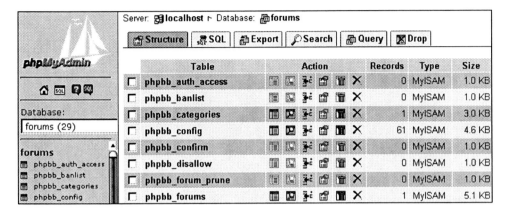

1. Click the **Export** tab to be taken to a page that looks like the following:

2. You can see all the tables in this database listed under Export in the top-left corner. Here you can individually select which tables to dump. Click Select All to dump all tables.

3. Leave all other fields at their default values. Double-check to see that both Structure and Data checkboxes are selected.

4. Select the Save as file checkbox.

5. Click Go.

6. You'll be prompted with a file dialog window asking under what name and where to save the dump file. Use mydump.sql as the filename and save it where you think most appropriate (for example, a directory designed to contain all your backup dumps).

What Just Happened?

You've successfully created an SQL dump file of all the tables and data found in your board database. In step 2 you saw an example of how you can selectively pick which tables to include in the dump and this way create several smaller dumps that together hold all the database tables and data.

If you now click on the ⚏ SQL tab, you'll be taken to a page that allows you to execute SQL queries.

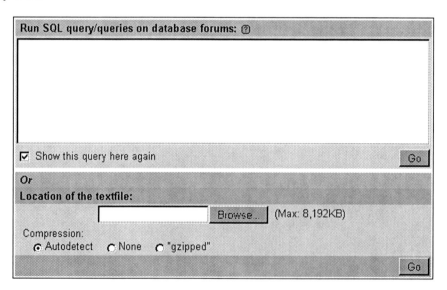

In the second half of the screenshot, under Location of the textfile title, you can upload a SQL dump to be executed into your database. This is the "restore" part of the operation. It's usually done on a completely different server and a blank database (for example, when you switch hosting providers and move your board).

In the case shown in the illustration, you see that there is a limit of 8192KB (or 8MB); you cannot upload dumps bigger that this. If your SQL dump is larger, you have to split it into smaller chunks. Another good option would be to explain the situation to your provider (they might suggest that you FTP the file and they can take it from there and import it using tools like the command-line MySQL utilities.

Using MySQL Command-Line Tools

If you have access to MySQL from the command line, huge databases won't be a problem; you should be able to do your backups and to restore if needed. Chapter 2 already discussed connecting to MySQL from the command line, using the `mysql` utility. Here we discuss another utility: `mysqldump`.

Creating Backups with mysqldump

As the name suggests this is a utility for creating SQL dumps from a MySQL database. It has a lot of options that you can always investigate by calling the utility with the `--help` option, like this:

```
mysqldump --help
```

You can also read about this utility at `http://dev.mysql.com/mysqldump`, the MySQL online manual.

Here's an example of how to use the utility for creating a dump of your `forums` database:

```
mysqldump -u dbuser -pdbpass forums > mydump.sql
```

This line in plain English means "Create an SQL dump of the database called `forums` and write this dump to a file called `mydump.sql`, located in the current directory. To prove that I'm allowed to access this database, I give you my username, which is `dbuser`, and my password, which is `dbpass`." Make note that the option -p and the password are glued together; there is no space like that between the -u option and the username.

If you have access on the server to create a scheduled task (a **cronjob**), you can have this command line executed daily for a fresh database copy. This command may vary depending on your server, mainly in the part after the right angle bracket, where the dump filename and its location are specified.

You can even go one step further and save hard-drive space by creating a compressed SQL dump and deleting the original dump, which can be large. On Linux systems you can use the `tar` archiver; the whole command that you can run as a cronjob would be something like:

```
mysqldump -u dbuser -pdbpass forums > mydump.sql ; tar cz mydump.sql -f
mydump.tgz ; rm -f mydump.sql
```

Now *that* is some real sysadmin-ing! Again if you want to translate this into plain English, it would mean "Create a SQL dump of my forums database and write it into mydump.sql. Compress mydump.sql and create mydump.tgz. Now delete the unneeded mydump.sql."

Using the mysql Utility to Restore a Database

To restore a database means to create a new database out of an existing SQL dump. Now that we have a mydump.sql that contains everything from the forums database, let's create a new database called forums-copy and have the contents copied there. You can do this in phpMyAdmin, but we'll see how to do it from the command line.

Time For Action—Creating a Database Copy from a SQL Dump

1. In the command line, type
    mysql -u dbuser -pdbpass
    and hit *Enter*.

2. Type CREATE DATABASE 'forums-copy';
    Hit *Enter*.

3. Type \u forums-copy.
    Hit *Enter*.

4. Type \. mydump.sql
    Hit *Enter*. If everything is fine, you'll see a lot of messages like this one:
    Query OK, 1 row affected (0.00 sec)

What Just Happened?

1. You connected to the database server.
2. You created a new database.
3. You selected the new database (forums-copy) to use it for the next operations.
4. You executed the mydump.sql file. Here you may need to adjust the path to the file, depending on where it's located.

Other Tools

Sometimes you may not use the command line MySQL tools or phpMyAdmin. Or the hosting provider's restrictions may make phpMyAdmin unusable for your huge dump. Don't despair, there's still hope! You can use some specially designed tools to deal with large databases. One such good tool is called BigDump, and can be downloaded free of charge from http://www.ozerov.de/bigdump.php.

It works around the server restrictions by taking small parts of your dump and executing them chunk by chunk until all the SQL commands are executed.

The Board's Human Side: Flamewars and Banning

Let's take a break from the sysadmin stuff and end this chapter with a look at the human side of running an online community. There are situations that you're most likely to encounter, which happen to almost every board admin, so it's good to be prepared or at least be aware that you're not alone.

Whatever your board is about, it's likely that it starts as a small board with a handful of nice fellows posting in it. Maybe the board will be an addition to your existing site; its forums might discuss the content of your site, where you'll answer questions and get suggestions.

If you happen to have a site with interesting content, your community is likely to grow gradually. As more and more people join in, more and more different opinions will be shared. An occasional flamewar can burst out, where some community members start exchanging hostilities. Do not panic! It's not you or your board or your site that is to blame for the flamewars. They just happen. They have been happening since the dawn of online communication, in Usenet groups, mailing lists, and so on. Flamewars are a part of the online communities; it's a human thing.

There can also be some community members that seem to like starting off new flamewars and look like they come to the board with the sole purpose of making the life of your community miserable. It happens. The anonymity provided by the Internet can make some folks behave quite differently from what they really are. You'll have to learn to live with this fact. But that doesn't mean that you'll have to tolerate such behavior. Some respected and valued community members may start limiting their participation and even leave the community for good, because of the bad behavior of those folks. This is something you don't want to happen.

It's tough in such situations, and there's no recipe. You have to use your best judgment, and have to act like a leader and an example for your community. At some point you'll probably end up writing sticky postings like "Read me before you post", sort of terms of use. This is a good and a necessary step because it sets the ground rules. Without rules there's no right or wrong; everybody can have a different understanding of what is acceptable behavior and what is not. You also need to be careful when writing these rules so as not to make them too restrictive. These rules need to be respected, that's why they are rules. So don't set impossible goals and wishlist items as rules; be a realist.

At some point the board may grow so much that you won't be able to follow what is happening all the time. You need someone to keep an eye on it. That's where moderators come into the picture. They are your best helpers with the board. They will volunteer their time to make the forums a better place for peaceful discussions. So choose them carefully. First, you have to trust your moderators. But chances are you've never even met those people; how can you trust them? Again, follow your gut feeling and use your best judgment.

Banning users is never an easy task. Try to avoid this as much as possible, because a banned user can find a way to register again and again using fake IP addresses and will keep abusing your community. And a banned user will be feeling and acting like a victim. So again, try to avoid banning as much as you can. Try to resolve any issues in a peaceful manner, try to listen to that user's problems and use banning as a last resort. But when you make the decision to ban someone, do it and be firm.

Here are some more tips that can help you with the board administration.

- Create a Private [Hidden] forum for your moderators. Let them talk about forum issues in privacy and make collective decisions.

- Create a Private [Hidden] forum that will serve as a recycle bin. Instead of deleting a thread, move it there. When only a few postings are to be deleted, but otherwise the topic is OK, split the postings in question to a new topic of their own and move this topic to the bin. The bin helps you have a history of what happened in case you need it. Grant your moderators access to the bin so that they can manage the topics moved there.

- When some board admins ban users, they do this temporarily and unban the troublemakers after let's say a week. Sometimes this helps.

- Users will complain about different things—you, the board, other users, and whatnot. Listen to what they have to say. But remember: there are a lot more people that are happy with the board, life, and everything. It's a normal behavior—when you're OK, you don't write a posting to say you're OK, but when you're angry about something, you write about it at once.

- Read the Netiquette book by Virginia Shea. It's available online at `http://www.albion.com/netiquette/book/`. It was written quite some time ago and it speaks about flamewars in Usenet groups and not in bulletin boards. So it's even more reassuring to see that you're not alone and your board is not the first one to experience such extremities. You'll recognize quite a few of your community members and situations described there and this is guaranteed to give you a good laugh. Such topics as the types of flames ("The Spelling Flame", "The Get-a-Life Flame") are really amusing.

- Again, there are no recipes, all the boards are different and unique, so use your best judgment and … be a leader. Good luck!

Index

F

Find action, modification action, 116
flamewars, 159
forum
    categories, 68
    creating, 68
    customization, 85
    deleting, 72
    display order, 73
    editing, 72
    elements, adding, 124
    flamewars, 159
    hacks, 110
    hidden forums, 152
    languages, adding, 125
    languages, support, 127
    management, 68
    MODs, 110
    permissions, 142
    permissions, setting up in Advanced Mode, 143
    permissions, setting up in Simple Mode, 74, 144
    private forum, 145
    pruning, 75
    searching, 52
forum customization. See phpBB styles
ForumPlasma gaming community, 12
forums. *See* communities

G

GaiaOnline community, 13
group permissions, 151
groups. *See* usergroups

H

.htaccess protection, 35
hidden forums, 152

I

image set, style element, 87
In-line actions, modification actions, 119

K

Keenspot bulletin board, 11

L

language support, 127

M

mass emailing, 77
memberlist, 55
MOD, permission level, 143
moderator. *See also* administrator
    assigning moderator privileges, 58
    postings, 59
    topics, 62
    user experience, 57
MODs. *See* phpBB modification
MS Outlook Task. *See* Tasks

N

netiquette, 160

O

online communities. *See* communities
Open action, modification action, 115

P

.pak files
    about, 136
    adding smilies, 136, 137
    creating, 138
    importing, 137
permissions, 68
    Advanced Mode, 143
    group permissions, 148, 151, 152
    levels, 143
    simple mode, 74, 144
    specifying for individual forums, 146
    types, 142
    type-to-level relationship, 144
    understanding, 146
phpBB
    about, 6
    administration, 127
    advantages, 7
    avatars, 34
    communities, example, 9
    configuring, 31

S

shell client, 21
simple mode, 74
smilies
    .pak file, 136, 137, 138, 139
    about, 78, 132
    adding, 135
    administration, 78
    Administration Panel, 134
    custom smilies, 136
    editing, 135
    importing, 137
    properties, 133
spam, 77
SQL action, modification action, 114
SQL database dump, creating, 155
sticky, permission type, 142
style elements, 86
styles. *See* phpBB styles
subSilver, default phpBB style, 85, 94

T

template, style element, 86
theme, style element, 86, 101
troubleshooting
    styles, 92

U

user experience, administrator
    Administrator Panel overview, 67
    database backup, 76
    database restore, 77
    forum administration, 68
    forum permissions, setting up in Simple
        Mode, 74
    forum, pruning, 75
    mass emailing, 77
    permissions, 68
    Resync option, 73
    smilies, 78
    user management, 79
    word filter, 78
user experience, moderator
    assigning moderator privileges, 58
    defining a moderator, 57
    forum, creating, 63

Moderator Control Panel, 65
    postings, editing and deleting, 59
    postings, managing, 59
    topics, locking, 63
    topics, managing, 62
    topics, moving to another forum, 63
    topics, splitting, 64
user experience, visitor
    logging in, 39
    memberlist, 55
    overview, 37
    posting, 44
    private messages, sending/receiving, 52
    profile, creating, 40
    profile, editing, 40, 41
    registering, 38
    replying, 45
    searching the forum, 52
    subscribing, 55
    usergroups, 56
    voting in polls, 54
user management
    Ban Control, 82
    banning, 82
    creating, 40
    deleting, 80
    disallowing usernames, 83
    editing, 79
    permissions, 81
    ranks, assigning, 139
user profiles. See user management
usergroups, 56
    about, 148
    creating, 149
    editing, 150
    permissions, 151
    permissions, setting, 152
    types, 148

V

view, permission type, 142
visitor
    user experience, 37
vote, permission type, 142

W

word filters/censors, 78

Printed in the United States
151247LV00003B/25/A